Intern Prog[rams as]
a Human R[esour]ces
Management Tool
for the Department
of Defense

Susan M. Gates

Christopher Paul

Prepared for the Office of the Secretary of Defense

Approved for public release, distribution unlimited

 NATIONAL DEFENSE RESEARCH INSTITUTE

The research described in this report was sponsored by the Office of the Secretary of Defense (OSD). The research was conducted in the RAND National Defense Research Institute, a federally funded research and development center supported by the OSD, the Joint Staff, the unified commands, and the defense agencies under Contract DASW01-01-C-0004.

Library of Congress Cataloging-in-Publication Data

Gates, Susan M., 1968–
    Intern programs as a human resources management tool for the Department of
Defense / Susan M. Gates, Christopher Paul.
      p. cm.
    Includes bibliographical references.
    "MG-138."
    ISBN 0-8330-3569-X (pbk. : alk. paper)
    1. United States—Armed Forces—Civilian employees. 2. United States. Dept. of
Defense—Officials and employees. 3. United States. Dept. of Defense—Personnel
management. 4. Civil service—Study and teaching (Internship)—United States. I.
Paul, Christopher, 1971– II.Title.

    UB193.G385 2004
    355.6'1969—dc22

                                                2004003570

The RAND Corporation is a nonprofit research organization providing objective analysis and effective solutions that address the challenges facing the public and private sectors around the world. RAND's publications do not necessarily reflect the opinions of its research clients and sponsors.

RAND® is a registered trademark.

Published 2004 by the RAND Corporation
1700 Main Street, P.O. Box 2138, Santa Monica, CA 90407-2138
1200 South Hayes Street, Arlington, VA 22202-5050
201 North Craig Street, Suite 202, Pittsburgh, PA 15213-1516
RAND URL: http://www.rand.org/
To order RAND documents or to obtain additional information, contact
Distribution Services: Telephone: (310) 451-7002;
Fax: (310) 451-6915; Email: order@rand.org

Preface

The Department of Defense (DoD), along with other federal agencies, is facing the need to substantially improve its workforce's effectiveness and efficiency and to address looming personnel challenges, such as how to deal with the imminent retirement of a large proportion of its civilian workers. In addition, the impending transformation of the U.S. military means that DoD's civil service workforce will likely have to meet new requirements in support of a new force structure.

Attracting and retaining sufficient civil service personnel of the highest caliber and with the appropriate and necessary skills are major DoD objectives. Approaches for achieving these aims are laid out in the DoD Civilian Human Resources Strategic Plan. One goal emphasized in this plan (Annex B) is "to promote focused, well-funded recruiting to hire the best talent available." An objective under this goal seeks to determine what type of internship will most effectively help DoD meet this goal.

DoD asked the RAND Corporation to characterize current intern programs in DoD, to identify best practices for intern programs among private-sector corporations and other government agencies, and to recommend approaches for improving such programs. As part of this effort, RAND conducted interviews with managers of several DoD intern programs to understand how current DoD programs work, and with managers of corporate programs to understand how those programs differ from the ones in DoD.

This monograph documents the project's findings. It presents the results of a review of literature on intern programs, insights obtained from interviews with managers of DoD and private-sector intern programs, findings from analyses of personnel data, and policy recommendations for DoD.

This monograph will be of interest to officials responsible for DoD recruiting and to those responsible for recruiting in other government agencies. It should also be of interest to DoD functional communities, human resource specialists and policymakers, and managers in other organizations.

This research was conducted for the Deputy Assistant Secretary of Defense for Civilian Personnel Policy. It was carried out within the Forces and Resources Policy Center of the RAND Corporation's National Defense Research Institute, a federally funded research and development center sponsored by the Office of the Secretary of Defense, the Joint Staff, the unified commands, and the defense agencies. Reader comments should be sent to the authors at the RAND Corporation, P.O. Box 2138, Santa Monica, CA 90407-2138, or to sgates@rand.org. The director of the program under which this research was conducted is Susan Everingham, who can be reached at the same RAND Corporation mailing address, at Susan_Everingham@rand.org, or at 310/393-0411, x7654. Information about the RAND Corporation can also be obtained at www.rand.org.

The RAND Corporation Quality Assurance Process

Peer review is an integral part of all RAND research projects. Prior to publication, this document, as with all documents in the RAND monograph series, was subject to a quality assurance process to ensure that the research meets several standards, including the following: The problem is well formulated; the research approach is well designed and well executed; the data and assumptions are sound; the findings are useful and advance knowledge; the implications and recommendations follow logically from the findings and are explained thoroughly; the documentation is accurate, understandable, cogent, and temperate in tone; the research demonstrates understanding of related previous studies; and the research is relevant, objective, independent, and balanced. Peer review is conducted by research professionals who were not members of the project team.

RAND routinely reviews and refines its quality assurance process and also conducts periodic external and internal reviews of the quality of its body of work. For additional details regarding the RAND quality assurance process, visit www.rand.org/standards/.

Contents

Figures and Table

Figures

Table

Summary

The Department of Defense (DoD) expects the number of its retiring civil service employees to increase over the next five years as a large portion of the civil service workforce becomes eligible for retirement. In addition to the effect that this exit of so many employees will have on DoD hiring demands, the Defense Transformation for the 21st Century Act—proposed defense legislation calling for a realignment of DoD's organizational structure and skill mix to address current objectives for the future and for the transfer to civilian personnel of some functions now performed by military personnel—has the potential to increase DoD's hiring demands even further.

Many within DoD are concerned about how the department and its components will find qualified individuals to replace such a large number of retiring employees and to fill available positions. At the same time, such a turnover in the workforce provides DoD with an opportunity to realize workforce planning goals—that is, to compare the skill mix of the current workforce with the skills needed to support tomorrow's military and then to make needed adjustments.

The DoD Civilian Human Resources Strategic Plan identifies intern programs as a potentially useful recruiting tool. To understand how DoD might use such programs most effectively, the Office of the Secretary of Defense asked the RAND Corporation to investigate the use of intern programs in DoD and other organizations, to gather information on effective practices and organizational options used in these programs, and to provide recommendations on DoD's use of intern programs. To address these issues, we conducted both a literature and an Internet review, as well as in-person interviews with representatives of private- and public-sector organizations.

Many Options Exist for Intern Programs

Our research focused on two categories of intern programs: pre-employment programs and structured post-employment programs, the latter of which we refer to as *early career professional development* (ECPD) programs.

Within the category of pre-employment internships, we looked at three kinds of programs: *summer internships,* defined as those employing students full-time during summer breaks and usually lasting between 8 and 12 weeks; *part-time internships,* defined as those employing students in the "off hours" during the school year or during breaks from school; and *co-op programs,* defined as those offering students continuous on-the-job experience, typically in a factory-oriented or technical job, over a period of months or years as the students complete their schooling. While all of these pre-employment internships provide multiple benefits when used successfully, they are primarily used as recruiting and screening tools.

The second category is ECPD programs, which are structured professional development programs designed for new hires. Their goal is to provide new employees with organization-specific training that will improve their ability to do their jobs and/or groom them for advancement to higher-level positions. Participants in DoD ECPD programs hire in at an entry level (usually GS-5, 7, or 9) and are non-competitively promoted to a higher, "target" grade level when they complete the program requirements. In the private sector, some companies, such as Ford Motor Company and Cigna, strongly emphasize ECPD for entry-level professional positions, involving most if not all new employees in structured ECPD programs.

DoD Emphasizes Early Career Professional Development Programs

We found examples of every kind of intern program within DoD, but ECPD programs are by far the most common. In fact, they are the only intern programs currently referred to by DoD as *internships*. ECPD program participants are hired into permanent, career-conditional civil service positions through either traditional civil service hiring practices or one of a handful of special hiring authorities. Pre-employment internships exist in DoD but are not common; summer internships are especially rare.

DoD can use two federal programs, both within the Student Educational Employment Program (SEEP), for hiring pre-employment interns. The first of these, the Student Temporary Employment Program (STEP), allows agencies to hire students on a part-time or short-term basis to get work done. The second, the Student Career Experience Program (SCEP), is oriented more toward training and development and is designed to groom students for term or permanent positions by providing them with work experience related to their educational program and career goals.

The Literature Identifies Successful Practices for Intern Programs

A substantial body of literature exists on the characteristics that successful pre-employment internships have in common.[1] Most of this literature draws lessons from the experience of private-sector organizations whose intern programs are well regarded and contribute to corporatewide hiring goals. One theme running through the literature on internships is to do them well or not at all.

Our review also identified several specific practices used by successful firms. We found three key guidelines for the recruitment and selection of participants for pre-employment internships:

---

[1] These characteristics are often referred to as *best practices* in the literature.

- **Carefully consider the organization's needs to ensure that potential candidates are a good fit.** If an organization's goal is to recruit permanent employees, it does not want interns it would not consider for permanent positions.
- **To attract the desired students, know what students are looking for.** While organizations need to understand their own goals for internship programs, they also need to know what potential participants expect to gain from the programs.
- **Identify effective means of gaining access to potential participants.** People learn about available internships through a variety of means, including Websites, job fairs, career preparation courses, and word of mouth.

We also identified several guidelines related to the management of pre-employment interns during the program:

- **Select good mentors.** Good mentorship and supervision are advocated as the best way to guide students' development and to give students a positive impression of the organization.
- **Provide students with interesting work.** Interns want to feel that they are not only contributing, but getting a real sense of what goes on in the company and what it is actually like to work there.
- **Provide benefits.** Even an unpaid internship becomes more appealing if there are tangible benefits such as assistance with relocation or housing, transportation, etc.
- **Administer the program carefully.** Ongoing engagement with both senior management and operational managers is important to ensure that program awareness is high, program objectives are being met, and areas for improvement are identified. Program administrators should also be encouraged to respond to problems quickly.
- **Be recruitment-minded throughout the program.** Being recruitment-minded starts with careful selection of candidates and extends to thoughtful monitoring and evaluation of their progress as interns.

Although there is no distinct literature describing best practices for ECPD programs, we were able to draw some useful observations from our review of literature on pre-employment intern programs. One finding is that ECPD programs are not a substitute for pre-employment intern programs. Private-sector organizations that use both kinds of programs typically use pre-employment internships as a screening tool to determine the best candidates for their ECPD programs, which they then use to train entry-level employees up to journeyman levels of competency. Another finding is that although ECPD programs focus less on recruitment and more on professional development than pre-employment internships do, they should still include thoughtful mentoring and rotational assignments.

Implications of Literature Review for DoD

A common theme running through the literature on effective practices for intern programs is the importance of keeping organizational goals in mind when designing and administering an intern program, whether of the pre-employment or ECPD kind. A clear understanding of program goals is especially critical in selecting participants and evaluating their work as interns. Since recruiting is a primary goal of pre-employment intern programs, substantial care typically goes into "selling" a student on the organization during the internship.

There are also costs associated with running an effective intern program. Pre-employment internships require a considerable investment of time and other resources, a point that organizations clearly take into account when deciding whether to use such a program and in selecting the kind of program to use.

A Program's Organization and Structure Influence Its Success

Issues such as who funds a program, who does the recruiting and hiring, and who evaluates interns can greatly influence a program's success in achieving its goals. We examined organizational options used for pre-employment intern and ECPD programs, deriving several conclusions about the structure and organization of intern programs both within and outside DoD.

Degree of Centralization Reflects Program Goals in Successful Intern Programs

In successful intern programs of all types, the funding, evaluation, and hiring decisions are made at the organizational level that is the focus of the program's objectives. In other words, programs designed to benefit the organization as a whole tend to receive high-level support and funding, as well as corporate input on hiring decisions. Similarly, programs whose purpose is to improve recruiting in or for a specific line of business or operational unit tend to be decentralized to the level of that operating unit. Intermediate degrees of centralization to the level of an organizational department consisting of several operational units or to the level of a functional community (e.g., a community of one or more related occupations) that cuts across many operating units of the organization are also possible.

Both ECPD and pre-employment intern programs may be used to achieve goals at any organizational level. ECPD programs typically have broad firm- or agencywide goals, and centralization or functionally based decentralization is the norm for these programs. But this does not mean that it is impossible to design a decentralized ECPD program to address the goals of an organizational subunit. Pre-employment internships typically have a combination of firmwide and narrower, business-line goals. Pre-employment intern programs are sometimes centralized, but most tend to be decentralized, often with actual program training content left to the discretion of operational managers, who may or may not receive significant centralized guidance. In both DoD and the corporate world, part-time intern programs and co-op programs are decentralized and locally driven, with funding usually derived from local budgets and personnel authorizations, although there is pressure for greater centralization.

Different Levels of Organizational Goals Imply Different Incentives

The incentive structures of successful pre-employment and ECPD programs are well aligned with the relevant level of organizational goals. For example, programs designed to meet corporatewide goals draw their primary input from individuals who can benefit from this corporate perspective. To operational unit managers, corporate goals may seem distant and abstract, so if the input of these managers is important to the program, incentives for their participation (e.g., centralized funding of intern program participants, centralized funding for mentors) may be required.

The degree to which an intern program is centralized can affect the breadth of goals. Centrally funded programs take a higher organizational view, preparing interns for a variety of positions in the company or developing "future leaders"; corporate exposure is likely to be broader, and "success" is measured in terms of an intern's migration to *any* permanent position in the company. Local or functionally funded internships, in contrast, are more likely to correspond (though they need not necessarily do so) with parochial training and goals. The experience and training an intern receives are likely to be narrower and more locally specific, and "success" for a location or function is the intern's migration to permanency *in that location or function.*

A Moderate Degree of Centralization Appears to Be a Successful Approach for Funding Intern Programs

One clear conclusion from our research is that the locus of funding for an intern program drives or is reflective of program objectives. It appears that some moderate level of centralization is the most effective option for funding internships. Local operational managers already bear the cost of mentoring or working with pre-employment intern or ECPD program participants, so being asked to pay the direct costs of such programs would put an additional burden on them. A functionally oriented and funded pre-employment intern or ECPD program provides the broader, functional community some ownership over and responsibility for program participants. A functional community is also better able than a local manager to deal with the risks and uncertainty involved in workforce planning and to adopt a perspective that considers the objectives of the organization as a whole rather than just those of an organizational subunit.

Larger, More Centralized Programs Tend to Have More-Comprehensive Mechanisms for Program Evaluation

Our research suggests that the larger, more centralized programs tend to have more-comprehensive, or formal, forms of program evaluation in place. This may reflect the fact that economies of scale accompany such evaluations in large programs, and that it is difficult to justify the expense of such evaluations for smaller programs. Another reason that smaller programs might not have formal program evaluation is that informal evaluation can suffice for their smaller scale.

Regardless of whether program evaluation is formal or informal, however, it tends to focus on cost and some measure of how well the program is achieving its objectives. For pre-employment intern programs, the outcomes of interest are the percentage of interns who receive a permanent job offer and, of those, the percentage who accept. ECPD programs tend to focus on the differences in retention rate and relative career success between program participants and employees who are similar but did not participate in the program.

Well-Regarded Intern Programs Are Part of a Human Resources Structure Designed to Meet Organizational Goals

Although there is ample literature describing specific practices used by successful intern programs, it appears that success may have more to do with the way programs are structured and with high-level support for such programs rather than with the use of specific practices. Well-regarded intern programs are part of a human resources (HR) structure that is designed to serve the organization's overall aims. Successful programs are not exclusively owned and run by HR, however. Instead, they are supported by HR and receive significant input and funding from functional communities and operational managers. This finding is consistent with the more general recommendations of the Strategic Human Capital Management approach, which suggests that government agencies emphasize human capital management and use the input of managers at all levels to design programs targeted to help the organization achieve its overall goals (General Accounting Office, 2002).

Centralization issues can be resolved in a variety of ways, all of which call for some, but not all, activities to be centralized. It appears that successful intern programs centralize only those activities that can benefit from economies of scale—such as the design of evaluation standards and tools, training materials for mentors, and general guidelines for structuring the intern programs. It is also common for organizations to centralize their contacts with colleges and universities to some degree. However, functional communities and/or operational units typically play a key role in identifying demand for interns (usually based on some medium-term forecasting of personnel needs in the functional area), selecting interns, designing the intern experience, and evaluating intern performance.

DoD Lacks the Hiring Flexibility Found in the Private Sector

The extent to which DoD can or should adopt organizational options used in other organizations is limited in certain respects. One key way in which private companies benefit from intern programs is that they are able to evaluate program participants and make offers of employment to the most successful of them. DoD, in contrast, cannot currently act on all the participant information available through its summer intern programs. SCEP allows for direct conversion to term or permanent positions, but only after a program participant has put in 640 hours—or 16 full-time weeks—of service with a federal agency. Because most summer programs last only 10 weeks, or 400 hours, a student who spends one successful summer in a DoD internship is not eligible for direct conversion.

Recommendations

The findings from our analysis suggest several ways for DoD to make more effective use of its intern and early career professional development programs.

First, in an effort to more effectively recruit recent college graduates, DoD should develop and employ terminology for describing different programs and positions that is free from DoD-

specific jargon and consistent with terminology used in the private sector. Specifically, DoD should consider eliminating the use of the term *intern program* to describe bona fide, permanent jobs that involve a substantial amount of professional development. Students, particularly those not familiar with the federal government, will tend to assume that an internship is not a "real job." We use the term *early career professional development* (ECPD) program to describe such jobs. DoD should consider adopting this or similar terminology.

Second, to the extent that DoD seeks to use pre-employment internships as a recruiting tool, it should create high-quality programs that maximize the potential for hiring talented interns as permanent employees. The SCEP hiring authority gives managers an opportunity to use pre-employment intern programs in a way that is consistent with how the private sector uses them—that is, as hiring and screening tools. DoD should bear in mind the lessons from the private sector on successful pre-employment internships. In particular, if the goal of these programs is to improve entry-level recruiting, DoD must be sure to design interesting work experiences with well-prepared, attentive mentors in order to make a positive impression on participants.

Expanded use of pre-employment intern programs should acknowledge recruiting as a primary goal and be closely linked with overall HR objectives. In creating new programs or expanding existing programs, DoD must balance local and departmentwide needs and link its decisions with larger workforce planning goals. As we witnessed in the case studies, local and organizationwide intern programs often have different objectives. The implementation of new or expanded DoD pre-employment intern programs should reflect the practices that the private sector uses to implement such programs.

Third, if DoD intends to use the summer internship as a recruiting tool, we recommend that it advocate changes to the SCEP rules. DoD's use of relatively few summer internships (in comparison to the number used by the private sector) is a rational response on the part of DoD managers to the hiring authorities available to them. The current array of hiring authorities provides no option for offering a permanent job to a successful summer intern after one summer.

Such an intern can only apply through the regular, competitive hiring process that is open to all applicants. And even after the intern does so, the DoD manager may be forced by federal hiring rules to choose another candidate.

Current Student Educational Employment Program (SEEP) regulations provide flexibility for DoD managers to use summer intern programs to achieve a variety of HR objectives. However, current SCEP requirements limit the extent to which DoD managers can effectively use summer internships as a recruiting tool. There are many reasons for DoD to consider using summer intern programs as a recruiting tool—for example, they have the potential to attract a much broader pool of candidates than part-time internships or co-op programs do.

If DoD decides to increase its use of summer internships as a recruiting tool, it should advocate policy changes that reduce the number of hours required for direct-conversion eligibility under SCEP. Current SCEP rules allow managers at federal agencies, including DoD, to directly convert to term or permanent employment only those individuals who successfully complete 640 hours of service during their time as students. If this figure were reduced to 400—a criterion that could be met by a full-time summer intern in one summer—managers would have the choice of converting promising summer interns to term or permanent employment.

Fourth, we recommend that DoD promote closer links between pre-employment intern programs and ECPD programs. Many of the private-sector companies we examined use pre-employment internships as a means of identifying employees for ECPD programs. To the extent that both pre-employment intern and ECPD programs share the objective of identifying employees desired by the organization, it is useful to reinforce the connections between these two types of programs.

Finally, we recommend that DoD facilitate the evaluation of intern programs by gathering information on pre-employment intern and ECPD program participation as part of the DoD-wide civilian personnel master file. Using the civilian personnel master file, DoD can track the careers of any civil service employee. If intern program participants could be identified in the data set, conversion rates could be examined, and career progression, promotion rates, and retention rates for program participants could be compared to those for similar employees who did not participate in such programs. Such comparative analytic tools are already in use within some DoD services and agencies.

Acknowledgments

We would like to thank all of those who took the time to tell us about the intern program(s) run by their agency, department, or firm. This research would have been much more difficult without their willingness to share and their frank and open comments. We would thank each individual by name, but that would violate the confidentiality of our interviews. We are especially grateful to Engin Crosby for providing us with reports and data on the Army Career Intern Program.

We are indebted to our sponsors, Ginger Groeber and John Ehrbar of the Office of the Secretary of Defense, Personnel and Readiness (Civilian Personnel Policy). We appreciate their support in all aspects of the project, and their valuable feedback and guidance following interim presentations of our work in progress. We also benefited from comments and feedback from Lizanne Stewman, John Moseley, and Frank Hushek of the DoD Civilian Personnel Management Service.

We would like to specifically thank our RAND Corporation colleague Gretchen Thompson, whose industry contacts (and willingness to share them) gave us a definite leg up in our research. We also benefited from interaction with RAND colleagues Elaine Reardon, Tessa Kaganoff, and Phoenix Do. Steven Garber and Cheryl Marcum, also of RAND, provided thoughtful reviews that improved the final report.

We thank Maria Falvo and Donna White for their assistance with the administrative aspects of the field interview process, and

Judy Lesso, RAND librarian, for her help in assembling material for the literature review. Special thanks to Kristin Leuschner for her writing efforts, which were invaluable in communicating our findings in this final document. Any errors or omissions that remain are solely our responsibility as the authors.

Acronyms and Initialisms

ACTEDS	Army Civilian Training, Education and Development System
AFMC	Air Force Materiel Command
AMC	Army Materiel Command
CREST	Career Related Experience in Science and Technology
DCAA	Defense Contract Audit Agency
DCMA	Defense Contract Management Agency
DELPA	Developmental Entry Level Professional Accountants
DEU	delegated examining unit
DFAS	Defense Finance and Accounting Service
DISA	Defense Information Systems Agency
DLA	Defense Logistics Agency
DMDC	Defense Manpower Data Center
DO	Directorate of Operations
DoD	Department of Defense
DON	Department of the Navy
ECPD	early career professional development
ELPA	Entry Level Professional Accountant
FCG	Ford College Graduate
FMCC	Financial Management Career Center
FORMIS	Forces, Readiness and Manpower Information System

FY	fiscal year
GAO	General Accounting Office
GS	General Schedule
HP	Hewlett-Packard
HR	human resources
IASP	Information Assurance Scholarship Program
IS	information science
IT	information technology
NACE	National Association of Colleges and Employers
NCES	National Center for Educational Statistics
OMB	Office of Management and Budget
OPM	Office of Personnel Management
OSD	Office of the Secretary of Defense
PMI	Presidential Management Intern
SCEP	Student Career Experience Program
SEEP	Student Educational Employment Program
STEP	Student Temporary Employment Program
VRA	Veteran's Recruitment Appointment
WHS	Washington Headquarters Services

CHAPTER ONE

Introduction

Background

The Department of Defense (DoD) anticipates an increase in the number of civil service employees retiring over the next five years as a large portion of this aging workforce reaches retirement eligibility. The DoD downsizing of the 1990s was achieved with minimal involuntary separations through hiring freezes and layoffs of junior personnel. However, as a result of this strategy, the average age and experience level of the DoD workforce have increased dramatically since 1989 (Department of Defense, 2001; Levy et al., 2001).

In fiscal year (FY) 2001, nearly 90,000 DoD civil service employees were eligible for retirement. Many within DoD are concerned about how DoD will find skilled individuals to replace such a large number of retiring employees. At the same time, however, this workforce turnover gives DoD the opportunity to realize workforce planning goals that might otherwise be difficult to achieve. By comparing the skills and competencies of the current workforce (considering how these will change as the current workforce ages) with the skills and competencies needed to support tomorrow's military, managers can make needed adjustments as current employees retire.[1]

---

[1] Emmerichs, Marcum, and Robbert (2003a,b) emphasize that the skills of a workforce are constantly changing as the individual employees get older and acquire new skills. The crucial skills gap for organizations is the one between the skill mix of the current workforce aged forward to a crucial point in time and the skill mix that leaders anticipate will be needed to meet organizational goals at that point in time. We find that this subtle distinction is often overlooked in the workforce planning process.

In addition to these pressures on the DoD recruiting infrastructure, proposed DoD legislation—*The Defense Transformation for the 21st Century Act*—has the potential to further increase hiring demands. By realigning DoD's organizational structure and skill mix to address current objectives and by transferring some functions now performed by military personnel to civilian personnel, the transformation could require DoD to hire a substantial number of civil service employees.

The DoD Civilian Human Resources Strategic Plan identifies recruiting "the best talent available" into the civil service as a key objective. Intern programs have been identified as a potentially useful recruiting tool. Specifically, the Strategic Plan calls on DoD to determine the type of intern program that can best meet DoD needs (Department of Defense, 2001, 2003).

These DoD efforts can be viewed as one part of a much larger effort to promote a "strategic human capital management" perspective in federal government agencies (see, for example, General Accounting Office, 2003). This perspective, advanced by, among others, the General Accounting Office (GAO), the Office of Management and Budget (OMB), and the Office of Personnel Management (OPM), encourages federal agencies to view the individuals they employ as assets to be invested in (e.g., through training) and to consider the value of human capital possessed by the workforce as an important organizational asset. The strategic human capital management perspective also emphasizes the importance of aligning human capital management approaches with the overall mission of the organization. According to this perspective, decisions related to intern programs should be made in the context of a broad consideration of human capital approaches.

Objectives

To inform DoD's recruitment efforts, the Office of the Secretary of Defense (OSD) asked the RAND Corporation to investigate the use of intern programs in DoD and other organizations and to gather information on best practices and organizational options within these programs. This monograph summarizes our findings about intern programs in DoD, other government organizations, and private businesses, and provides recommendations regarding DoD's use of intern programs.

In examining the range of options available for DoD intern programs, we identified four distinct types. The first three types—summer internships, part-time internships, and co-op programs—fall under the heading of pre-employment programs. In summer internships, perhaps the most common type of pre-employment program, students are employed full-time during summer breaks. In part-time internships, students work either during the school year or during breaks from school. In co-op programs, which may involve part-time work during the school year or full-time work alternating with full-time coursework, students integrate their work experience with their degree program, often earning credit for the work they do.[2] The fourth type of intern program, the structured early career professional development (ECPD) program, is for new hires.

DoD currently uses all four kinds of intern programs in some way, but ECPD programs are the most common among its structured intern programs. The Army and Air Force both have large, centrally funded ECPD programs—the Army Career Intern Program, the Air Force Copper Cap Program, and the Air Force Palace Acquire Program. The Navy does not have a broad, centralized ECPD program, but its Navy Financial Management Traineeship provides ECPD opportunities for financial managers. Defense agencies also offer structured ECPD programs. The Defense Finance and Accounting Service (DFAS) has the Entry Level Professional Accountant (ELPA) pro-

---

[2] Our description of intern programs represents a generic typology that can be broadly applied to characterize programs in both the public and the private sector. The terminology used within a particular sector or specific organization to describe one or more of these options may vary, however. For example, our category of co-op programs could include the DoD's Student Career Experience Program (SCEP), even though the term *co-op* is not officially applied to this program within the DoD. (The term *co-op* does continue to be used unofficially within DoD, but there is no longer a specific co-op appointment.)

gram; the Defense Contract Management Agency (DCMA) and the Defense Contract Audit Agency (DCAA) each have their own ECPD programs.

In contrast to DoD's wealth of formal, centralized ECPD programs, its use of pre-employment intern programs is more ad hoc. DFAS recently initiated a summer intern program for accounting students. The Army Materiel Command (AMC) has a small pre-employment intern program called CREST (Career Related Experience in Science and Technology). DCAA runs pre-employment internships out of its five regional centers, the vast majority of its interns working part-time on a year-round basis. In addition to these small, decentralized programs that may span more than one location, local operational managers may use the Student Career Experience Program (SCEP) and Student Temporary Employment Program (STEP) hiring authorities to hire students. Although the relationship between the local manager and the student may look like a co-op or a part-time or summer internship, it may not be part of a formal intern program. DoD currently uses all forms of intern programs to some extent; what our study considered is whether DoD might benefit from a different mix of options.

To understand how DoD might benefit further from available intern program options, we identified practices used by organizations in the private and public sectors that are viewed as having successful intern programs. We also examined in detail the kinds of structures used to organize intern programs and considered the effect of organizational structures on program objectives and the types of programs most appropriate for meeting DoD goals. To provide additional insights, we highlighted specific case studies.

The intern programs we discuss are often closely aligned with more-general recruiting and professional development activities within organizations. Indeed, most intern programs function as recruiting and/or professional development strategies. We focus specifically on intern programs, without delving deeply into the more-general human resources (HR) functions of recruiting and professional development. Related RAND research for OSD is looking at recruiting practices more generally.

Although broad pressures exist for federal agencies to transform the way they think about workforce management and adopt a strategic human capital management approach, an explicit consideration of how intern programs would fit into (or should be transformed in accordance with) such a perspective is both premature and beyond the scope of our study. That said, many of the broad themes of the strategic human capital management approach—the need to invest in the workforce, to link hiring and training decisions to strategic planning efforts, and to target investments in human capital to where they are needed most—are echoed herein in the context of intern programs.

Methods

The research presented here is based on literature and Internet review, data analysis, and interviews. Our reviews of the literature and Internet sought to gather information on existing and past programs in DoD and other organizations, student perceptions of intern programs, and the practices used by organizations with successful intern programs. The Internet search involved a broad-based multi-engine search on *internship* and the following related keywords: *intern, experiential education, co-op, fellowship,* and *summer program.* This broad search was supplemented with directed searches of several universities' career center (or equivalent) Web pages and a careful inspection of Web materials available through NACE (National Association of Colleges and Employers). The broader literature review included searches on similar keywords in databases of business and academic journals and periodicals, and also entailed collecting articles and studies referred to in materials found during our "primary" search. These searches yielded a wide range of materials, including lists and evaluations of internship programs (see Oldman and Hamadeh, 2002), surveys of students or employers (see Gold, 2001, 2002, for example), advertisements for specific programs along with their details and applications, and a variety of lessons learned, advice for running, and best-practices lists from and for intern programs (see

Patterson, 1997; Brooks and Greene, 1998; or Cunningham, 2002, for example).

We conducted interviews with managers of DoD, other federal government, and corporate intern and co-op programs. Within DoD, we attempted to identify and interview managers of each service or agencywide intern program. To select DoD programs and private-sector firms for interviews, we used a referral/convenience method, usually referred to as "snowball sampling," in which we began with an initial list of contacts to get recommendations for additional contacts. For DoD programs, we began with a list of contacts provided by our sponsor. We then expanded from this initial list based on word-of-mouth referrals from individuals in our first round of contacts and from referrals from existing RAND contacts in various DoD agencies.

For private-sector contacts, we established a list of "best practice" firms based on our review of the literature and consultations with RAND HR personnel. We then attempted to contact all firms on the list having personnel who were members in HR professional organizations that RAND HR personnel were also members of. By using HR-to-HR referrals/contacts, we were able to successfully speak with a much higher proportion of the private-sector companies we tried to contact than would have been the case if we had resorted to cold-calling.

We were able to complete interviews with three of the four companies we initially selected as targets. Given that our catalog of HR-to-HR relationships produced a large list of potential contacts, we decided to select our target corporate case studies based on the following criteria. First, we focused on large corporations that employ individuals in many locations around the country and in occupational areas similar to those found in DoD. Second, to enable us to examine different strategies for structuring intern programs, we chose companies known by our internal HR contacts to use different approaches. Our interviews of these private-sector companies were used to gather information unavailable on Websites or in published documents on the operational details of intern programs.

Table 1.1 lists the government and private-sector organizations used in our case studies and identifies which types of internships we

Table 1.1
Case Studies

Organization	Pre-Employment Internships			ECPD
	Summer	Part-time[a]	Co-op	
Private sector				
Ford Motor Company	✓		✓	✓
Hewlett-Packard	✓	✓	✓	
Northrop Grumman	✓		✓	
Government				
Air Force[b]				✓
Army[b]				✓
Army Materiel Command	✓			✓
Defense Contract Audit Agency		✓	✓	✓
Defense Finance and Accounting Service	✓			✓
Department of the Navy Human Resources				✓
Central Intelligence Agency	✓	✓	✓	✓
Navy Financial Management				✓
Defense Contract Management Agency				✓

[a]A ✓ in this column indicates that the organization as a whole has a visible, formal, part-time internship program. If functional managers within the organization are hiring part-time interns out of their own budgets on an ad hoc basis without any reference to the larger agency or firm, we do not designate the organization as having a part-time intern program.
[b]The Air Force and Army case studies focus on the servicewide ECPDs (Palace Acquire, Copper Cap, and Army Career Intern Program) and do not reflect the full array of programs available in these services.

discussed with each organization. Fuller descriptions of these organizations can be found in Appendix A.

We used a semiformal open-ended structure for our interviews. See Appendix B for our interview protocol.

Additionally, we conducted a data review and analysis. We reviewed analyses conducted by the Army to forecast demand and evaluate the Army Career Intern Program. We used the DoD personnel database, FORMIS (Forces, Readiness and Manpower Information System), available from the Defense Manpower Data Center

(DMDC), to analyze data on student trainees in DoD. Finally, we analyzed questions related to internships in the National Center for Educational Statistics (NCES) Baccalaureate and Beyond Survey.[3]

Scope

There are significant limitations to the literature on best practices that should be mentioned here. First, the term itself is not well defined. As used in the literature, it can mean anything from "something that sounds like a good idea" to a specific, well-defined practice that has a proven correlation with the success of an organization. We must be up front in noting that the literature on best practices for intern programs does not accord with the latter description. Most of the work from which we drew our lessons identifies best practices by looking at the practices of organizations that are (1) known for having intern programs that are considered successful (i.e., are well regarded by students or have a high rate of conversion to full-time employment), (2) well regarded for their employment management practices, or (3) successful in their business as a whole. The literature can provide no concrete proof that these practices led to success of one kind or another. There is also no guarantee that practices that may have been ignored by this literature are not equally important. The organizations identified as best-practice organizations for our case studies are those that the HR professional community and/or college career advising professionals recognize as having effective programs. Again, there is no sense in which these organizations should be seen as "the best" in any specific, objective way compared to a set of other organizations.

One reason for the limited amount of objective concrete evidence on the relationship between specific practices and the success of intern programs is the difficulty in generating reliable and accurate measures of success for such programs. Obvious candidate measures,

---

[3] See http://nces.ed.gov/surveys/b&b.

such as promotion or hiring rates, suffer from important limitations that we discuss later.

Another key concern is whether practices viewed as effective for private-sector organizations are relevant to public-sector organizations such as DoD. We believe there are compelling reasons to think the answer is yes in this context. The federal government competes for workers in the same labor market as private-sector organizations do. One individual might very well entertain job offers from both types of organizations. In the late 1990s, employers faced an extremely competitive employment market and thus experienced tremendous pressure to experiment with new ways to improve their hiring outcomes. Private-sector organizations had more flexibility to experiment and react quickly than public-sector organizations did. Those that were able to recruit and retain high-quality employees through intern programs can be viewed as successful relative to organizations that were not able to do so.

In presenting information on effective practices, we have tried to emphasize the fact that the practices cannot be objectively defended as better than other practices. The practices we highlight are those that are general enough to apply to both private- and public-sector organizations, are recommended by more than one source, and appear to make good practical sense.

Document Overview

In Chapter Two, we describe the range of programs that have been categorized as internships and the objectives such programs can have, and discuss case study examples of different kinds of internships. We then evaluate DoD's current use of internships in relation to the range of what is available. In Chapter Three, we identify the effective practices for intern programs that we found in the literature.

In Chapter Four, we look in more detail at the four basic types of intern programs: pre-employment programs (summer and part-time internships, and co-ops) and ECPD programs. We also consider how programs are organized differently in the public and private sectors and how organizational structure influences the identification and implementation of program objectives. We then discuss the types of programs that appear to be most appropriate for meeting DoD goals. Chapter Five offers our conclusions and policy recommendations for DoD.

CHAPTER TWO

Types of Intern Programs

One issue we explored is the extent to which DoD is making full and effective use of existing internship options. In this chapter, we describe the range of intern programs in the public and private sectors, focusing particularly on the objectives of these programs. Case study examples, from within and outside DoD, are also provided.

We then turn our attention more fully to DoD programs. We describe DoD's experience in view of the range of available options and identify lessons for DoD.

Kinds of Internships

The term *internship* has a variety of meanings depending on the context. Figure 2.1 shows the distinctions we make among various types of programs that can collectively be called intern programs.

Figure 2.1
Different Types of Intern Programs

Prior to Full-Time Permanent Employment	During Full-Time Permanent Employment
Pre-employment intern programs • Co-op programs • Part-time internships • Summer internships	Early career professional development (ECPD) programs

RAND *MG138-2.1*

The first distinction we make is between programs involving full-time, permanent employees of an organization and those involving individuals who are not yet full-time permanent employees. We use the term *early career professional development* (ECPD) to refer to programs for full-time permanent employees. We use the term *pre-employment internship* to describe programs targeting people who are not yet full-time permanent employees of an organization. Pre-employment programs, sometimes referred to as *experiential education* programs, typically target students who are currently enrolled in formal education programs. Within the category of pre-employment internships, we further distinguish among summer internships, part-time internships, and co-op programs.

We next describe each kind of internship in more detail and provide case study examples to illustrate different options.

Pre-Employment Internships

Summer and part-time internships share many features. Both are typically of limited duration, often lasting just for the summer break or a single semester. Summer programs are, obviously, internships that students undertake during the summer school recess; most summer programs last between 8 and 12 weeks. Part-time internships involve students working at their internship in their "off hours," either on days or at times of day when they do not have classes. Jobweb (2002) defines part-time and summer internships as "a one-time work or service experience done by a student who has attained at least some academic preparation in a professional field. The student, who can be an advanced undergraduate or graduate student, works in a professional setting under the supervision of at least one practicing professional."

Students participating in summer or part-time internships may be paid by the organization sponsoring the internship and may receive academic credit. Wide variation exists in terms of the pay, academic credit, and perquisites (e.g., housing or travel expenses, benefits) associated with internships. Some sectors of industry tend to use internships that have—or lack—certain features; for example, internships in media are almost always unpaid, largely for union reasons, although they do give college credit.

Co-ops, a third type of pre-employment intern program, are less common than summer and part-time internships. In a co-op program, students acquire continuous on-the-job experience over a period of months or years while completing their schooling. Co-op programs are traditionally for factory-oriented or technical jobs. Some 75 percent of all co-op programs nationwide involve students working on engineering degrees (Patterson, 1997). Students participating in co-op programs are almost always paid and almost always receive academic credit.

Co-op programs bear a close resemblance to part-time intern programs but are usually more formal. Co-op students either alternate semesters between the internship and coursework (the classic co-op) or do both simultaneously. Unlike part-time internships, co-op programs *require* that the university the student attends be formally involved. Typically, the student, university, and place of employment collaborate to articulate the nature of the work experience and design some formal assessment process to ensure that the student is making progress and learning on the job.

Participation in Pre-Employment Internships

Pre-employment internships are very popular among college students. Nearly a third of college graduates participate in some form of pre-employment internship either while in school or immediately after. Although much of the information on internships and program participation is anecdotal, the Baccalaureate and Beyond Survey, conducted by the National Center for Educational Statistics (NCES), provides information on educational and work experiences, including the internship experiences of 11,000 college graduates who completed their baccalaureate degree in the 1992–93 school year. These students and their parents were interviewed in 1993; follow-up interviews with the students were conducted in 1994 and 1997. The 1993 data reveal that 28 percent of the students had a pre-employment internship during the 1992–93 school year or the previous summer. In addition to this 28 percent who reported holding an internship while enrolled in school, 14 percent of the students surveyed in 1997 reported having held an internship after graduation from college.[1] Of these, 14 percent were in co-op programs and 86 percent were summer or part-time interns.

We found that participating students came from a variety of academic majors. Most likely to participate were students majoring in architecture, ethnic studies, journalism, communications, computer programming and information science (IS), chemical engineering,[2] physical education, public health, paralegal studies, military science, environmental studies, leisure studies, physical sciences, social work, political science, sociology, and international relations.

Objectives of Pre-Employment Intern Programs

While pre-employment programs can supply firms with multiple benefits, their primary use is as a recruiting and screening tool. Crumbley and Sumners (1998) note that internships are a recruiting tool first, and that secondary benefits include enhanced selection and screening of potential candidates, development of positive relationships with local universities, and an improved image of the profession associated with the company. While corporate rhetoric may play up the social value of internships, at bottom, "employers recognize the value of experiential education programs in terms of recruitment and retention" (Gold, 2001). This view of internships may be a fairly recent (a decade or so old) development. "It used to be that an internship was just a summer job program. Now, more companies are seeing it as a way to develop potential hires" (Watson, 1995).

Pre-employment internships allow companies to learn about the qualities and "fit" of potential hires. Seventy percent of employers use internships to "test drive" job candidates (Gold, 2001). Intern pro-

---

[1] These internships might have occurred while the individual was enrolled in a graduate program.

[2] Interestingly, electrical and mechanical engineering students are about as likely to participate in pre-employment internship programs as the average student is, whereas students in civil engineering and other engineering majors are less likely.

grams enable an organization to develop a hiring pool with experience specific to the organization and provide the organization with new blood and fresh ideas.

Conversion rates are sometimes used as measures of the success of intern programs (Scott Resource Group, 1999). Cunningham (2002) suggests that a successful experiential education program will convert at least 50 percent of its graduating interns to full-time, permanent employees. Classic co-ops tend to have extremely high conversion rates to full-time, permanent employment, while part-time internships have a broader range of conversion rates. One study (Nagle and Collins, 1999) found that the "conversion rate" was 55.1 percent for co-ops, 52.5 percent for part-time interns, and only 20.1 percent for summer employees. Another study (Gold, 2001) found that "co-op employers reported making permanent employment offers to an average 65 percent of co-ops, with a 67.2 percent acceptance rate. Employers made offers to 56.9 percent of interns, 62.4 percent of which were accepted. An average of 57.5 percent of summer hires were offered jobs, and 62.9 percent accepted them."

Public- and private-sector organizations often have different practices with regard to hiring interns. Figure 2.2 shows results from a survey of firms offering experiential education programs (i.e., pre-employment intern programs) at the University of North Carolina, Chapel Hill, in 2001. As is evident, there is an important difference between sectors in the emphasis they place on summer internships versus part-time intern and co-op programs as a source of new hires. Whereas the public (nonprofit and government) sector hires more co-op and part-time students than summer interns, the reverse is true in the private sector (service and manufacturing industries). Another study (Brooks and Greene, 1998) found that in their sample of firms, for-profit companies offered an average of 55 percent of their summer interns permanent positions, compared to only 5 percent for not-for-profit companies. This suggests that not-for-profits and government organizations may be lagging the for-profit, private sector in the effective use of summer internships as a recruiting tool.

Figure 2.2
Recruitment from Experiential Education Programs Offered at the University of North Carolina, Chapel Hill, 2001

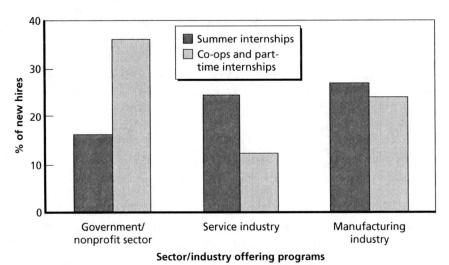

Organizations that have formal, structured ECPD programs view pre-employment intern programs as complements to those programs. Indeed, it appears that organizations with highly structured ECPD (in other words, those making a high level of investment in new employees) place a stronger emphasis on the importance of pre-employment internships as a recruiting and screening tool. For example, Ford Motor Company runs a centralized summer intern program that brings nearly all interns to the Detroit area. Interns are evaluated against a common set of metrics, and the most highly ranked interns receive job offers for positions in the Ford College Graduate (FCG) program at the end of the summer. Ford would like all FCG program hires to come from the ranks of summer interns. Similarly, the Cigna Website notes that most entry-level hires are former interns.

Case Study Example: Hewlett-Packard

Hewlett-Packard (HP) uses a variety of internship options.[3] In fact, any full-time student who works for HP is considered to be "an intern." HP's internship programs have two goals: to identify and bring high-quality talent into the company, and to provide anticipatory training to prospective new hires.

HP's main focus is its summer program, but the company also has part-time internship and co-op positions available, in much smaller numbers. The summer program is spread out through all of HP's geographic regions; HP has upward of 300 summer interns at its corporate headquarters and averages cohorts of 20 to 50 elsewhere (with cohorts of as few as one intern at its smallest locations).

HP also has a small number of part-time interns, who are brought in through the initiative of operational managers, and a small number of co-op students, who come from HP's relationships with universities. Neither of these programs receives the same level of corporate attention or support that the summer program does, but both provide additional flexibility and keep invested parties happy.

Case Study Example: Defense Finance and Accounting Service

Unlike many other DoD agencies, DFAS uses the term *intern program* to refer to a structured summer program for students. DFAS's summer intern program was developed by its accounting line of business, one of several lines of business, or organizational subunits, in DFAS. Students are hired through the SCEP hiring authority (described in more detail later). There were 32 participants in 2002, and more than 37 were planned for 2003. In addition to the summer intern program, DFAS has a handful of co-op students in the accounting line of business.[4]

The goal of the summer intern program is recruiting. DFAS tests out the candidates to see if they are a good fit, and the students

---

[3] For more information about Hewlett-Packard and other organizations referenced in the case studies, see Appendix A.

[4] Co-op students are also hired through SCEP.

also test out DFAS. DFAS managers believe it is crucial to provide students with a good experience so that they will want to work for the organization. Students are paired with seasoned accountants who have been carefully selected to serve as supervisors and mentors to the interns. In selecting these individuals, DFAS managers look for positive, upbeat people, the "superstars" who have not yet been promoted to supervisors. DFAS managers can benefit from the program in that interns can help free up managers' time for development activities. However, because the managers of the accounting line of business believe the intern program benefits the organization as a whole, it can be difficult to convince them to invest time and money in interns who leave at the end of the summer.

The intern program consists of 70 percent on-the-job training, 20 percent group projects, and 10 percent topical briefings and networking. Often interns are used as internal consultants; their group project will address some concern facing the business lines. The briefings are considered a marketing tool, to explain why DFAS is important; they also help build networks among the students. Social networks and group events are important parts of the intern program and a big reason for its appeal for students.

Early Career Professional Development Programs

The other form of internship we discuss is the ECPD program, which, broadly speaking, is a structured professional development program designed for new hires. The purpose of ECPD programs is to provide organization-specific training to new employees to improve their ability to do their jobs and/or to groom them for advancement to higher-level positions. The programs we looked at, in both DoD and the private sector, last between 18 and 36 months, after which time the employee is no longer part of the ECPD program. In DoD, agencies often describe those who have completed the ECPD program as "graduates" who have "transitioned to full performance positions." In contrast to pre-employment interns, ECPD interns are permanent employees, receiving the salary and benefits associated with the position they were hired into.

ECPD programs are common in the public sector, especially in DoD. Participants in DoD ECPD programs are hired through competitive civil service processes[5] into an entry-level position (usually GS-5, 7, or 9) and are noncompetitively promoted to a higher "target" grade level as they successfully complete the program requirements. The job posting for positions in such programs lists both the entry-level grade and the target, or "full-performance" grade level. DoD ECPD programs exist in organizations and functional areas having a well-defined career ladder, and the career ladder provides the structure around which the ECPD program is shaped. However, entry-level positions in a particular career ladder are not all part of an ECPD program.[6]

In the private sector, some companies, such as Ford Motor Company and Cigna,[7] strongly emphasize ECPD for entry-level professional positions, and involve most, if not all, new employees in structured ECPD programs. Many other companies emphasize the importance of training and development but do not offer broad, structured ECPD programs.

It should be noted that although DoD, and federal government agencies more generally, calls ECPD programs "internships," this is not common practice in the private sector. In fact, we did not find any private-sector organizations that called ECPD programs internships. For our purposes, however, we refer to all ECPD programs, whether run by public or private organizations, as internships.

---

[5] Allowable hiring authorities are discussed in greater detail later. In addition to the standard competitive rating and ranking process, special hiring authorities such as the Federal Career Intern Authority, Outstanding Scholars Program, and Veteran's Readjustment Authority, and direct conversion from SCEP may be available, depending on the position and the individual applying for it.

[6] Similarly, services and agencies differ as to whether all positions in a particular functional area are part of a functional career ladder. In the Army, there are 22 career fields, or programs, which cover 86,000 out of 220,000 civilian employees. If a job is in a numbered series covered by a career program, then the individual holding that job is part of that career program. However, in the Air Force, participation in career programs is voluntary, and only a fraction of positions in a particular career field are officially part of a career program.

[7] See http://www.cigna.com/general/working/development/current_programs.html.

Objectives of ECPD Intern Programs

Like pre-employment internships, ECPD internships seek to bring desirable employees into the organization. However, the goal of ECPD programs is typically not just to bring people into the organization, but also to train new employees for more-advanced positions. For example, DoD ECPD programs have the explicit goal of grooming new hires for more-advanced positions in the service or agency sponsoring the ECPD program. DoD interns are permanent employees; they are typically college graduates. They receive the standard salary and benefits associated with the grade level they are hired into.

Many of the ECPD programs in DoD exist because of a belief that it is difficult to hire people with the skills required for the journeyman-, or full-performance, level positions (usually GS-11 or GS-13). With these programs, people can be recruited into DoD at an entry level and provided with the on-the-job training needed to perform journeyman-level functions. In this sense, then, these programs relate to recruiting. However, we observed no explicit attempt to use ECPD programs in recruiting to portray a DoD organization as a forward-looking employer committed to employee development.

The private sector also uses ECPD programs to train employees for advancement. As mentioned above, companies such as Ford Motor Company and Cigna emphasize participation in ECPD programs. However, many companies provide professional advancement opportunities and training without the use of formal ECPD programs. For example, on their company Websites, PepsiCo and Northrop-Grumman describe a wide variety of professional development opportunities that are "available" to employees.[8] HP adopts an even more decentralized approach: "We invest heavily in the development of all our employees, but believe that everyone should drive their own development path. For this reason, we will encourage you to build an individual development plan to help identify your training needs and

---

[8] See, respectively, http://www.pepsicocareercenter.com and http://www.northropgrumman.com/careers/careers_main.html.

ensure they are met during an agreed-upon timeframe."[9] Structured
ECPD programs are sometimes offered by one or more lines of business but not companywide, as is the case at General Motors and
Honeywell.[10] DuPont offers ECPD programs in three of seven career
fields.[11]

Case Study Examples: Army Career Intern Program and Ford Motor Company

In both DoD and the private sector, we observed examples of highly
structured ECPD programs for entry-level professional hires. In each
case, the program's goal was to provide broad training to start new
hires on a path to leadership positions within the organization. The
Army Career Intern program is an example of such a program within
DoD. This program originated in 1974 and grew in size until the
mid-1980s. In 1985, 1,627 graduates of the program were placed in
journeyman-level positions. Army analysts have tracked the careers of
the interns and of the pool of individuals hired directly into comparable journeyman-level positions without taking part in the ECPD
program. Of the total number of individuals hired into these positions, the proportion of Army Career Intern program interns has
varied from a low of 19 percent in 1996 to a high of 61 percent in
1990. And between 1983 and 1993, the proportion was consistently
above 50 percent.

Over time, retention rates have been higher among program
graduates than among nongraduates, but how much higher depends
dramatically on the cohort considered and the number of years for
which retention is compared. For example, a comparison of the cohorts of graduates and the cohorts of nongraduates appointed to
journeyman-level positions in FY 1986 shows that career retention
rates for the former were 5, 13, and 23 percentage points higher con-

---

[9] See http://www.jobs.hp.com/content/training/training.asp?Lang=ENen&area=US.

[10] See, respectively,http://www.gm.com/company/careers/career_site.html and http://www.honeywell.com/careers/page3_2_4.html.

[11] See http://www.dupont.com/dupontglobal/corp/careers/working_development.html.

sidered after 1, 5, and 10 years, respectively. For the FY 1983 cohorts, however, the rates for the graduates were 0, 8, and 11 percentage points higher.

The Ford Motor Company provides an example of an ECPD program within the private sector. As described on the company's recruiting Website,[12] the program promises new employees mentorship, networking opportunities, and developmental assignments "that reflect your interests and the company's needs." The FCG program has a long history. The recruiting Website states: "In 1951, Henry Ford II launched the Ford Graduate Training Program to develop company leaders. Today, our Ford College Graduate program is a proven program that provides broad experience and training at the outset of your career."

Ford Motor Company makes a strong commitment to the professional development of entry-level hires into salaried positions.[13] From interviews with Ford personnel, we learned that about 30 percent of Ford's salaried hires come in at the entry level. Nearly all such hires are recent college graduates who are brought into the FCG program. Ford hires people as co-op students, interns, and entry-level hires (FCG program), and at mid-career and senior levels ("experienced professionals"). In 2002, due to economic conditions Ford hired only 1,600 salaried people. In a typical year, Ford hires 5,800 to 8,000.

The Ford program is similar to formal DoD ECPD programs. As described on Ford's recruiting Website, the company is divided into eight operational units, each with its own development program. The specifics of the FCG program are determined by the operational units, which design rotational assignments within the operational unit and then place participants in permanent positions. In general, however, participants in the FCG program must be "mobile"—that

---

[12] See http://www.mycareer.ford.com/CareerPrograms.asp.

[13] This discussion applies only to salaried positions. Hiring and training for hourly employees are decentralized to the plant level, and hourly employees do not participate in this ECPD program.

is, willing to go where the job opportunities are—or they will not stay with the company.

In most of the operational units, the program is for two years, although there is some variation across and even within units. For example, in manufacturing, the career development program can last up to five years in some specialties. These developmental programs include rotational assignments and skill development opportunities for new hires. Some (such as information technology [IT]) include cross-functional assignments in other operational units. There is a seven-week, hands-on "New Hire Orientation" for IT staff. All of the operational units assign mentors to program participants to guide them in selecting professional development assignments.

Retention of employees during the course of the FCG program is 90 to 95 percent. At this point, Ford does not track long-term retention of program participants, though there are plans to do so. In addition, Ford plans to track the time it takes participants to progress to entry-level management.

DoD and the Range of Internship Programs

Having examined different kinds of internship programs, including examples from DoD, we can now take a closer look at the extent to which DoD makes use of the range of programs offered.

Before we begin, we want to note that DoD often uses its own terminology to describe various kinds of internship opportunities. For example, until recently DoD used the term *co-op* to refer to the kinds of ongoing cooperative programs described earlier in the chapter as well as to participants in part-time pre-employment programs. Though no longer used officially to refer to any particular appointment, *co-op* continues to be used informally. In DoD, participants in summer programs, co-op programs, and other internships are usually referred to formally as *student trainees*.

ECPD Programs Are Far More Common Than Any Other Kind of Internship

ECPD programs are by far the most common kind of internship used in DoD, and they are the only kind of programs whose participants are regularly referred to as *interns*.

Most DoD ECPD program managers we spoke with reported that the local managers' demands for ECPD positions exceeded either the availability of these positions or the resources an organization had to support the positions. Some of this excess demand may be due to the fact that ECPD programs tend to be centrally funded, which means there is no direct personnel cost to the local unit. In other words, demand is high because the price of these participants is artificially low. However, this phenomenon does not account for all of the excess demand. We observed several organizations in which locally funded ECPD programs existed as a supplement to centrally funded programs. For example, the Army Career Intern program now has an end-strength of 1,000 work-years. Local managers are able to develop local intern programs for these entry-level positions as well. Currently, there are only about 100 locally funded ECPD participants; in the mid-1980s, however, that number was as high as 3,800.

Because most ECPD program participants are hired into DoD as permanent, career-conditional employees, there is no way to identify ECPD program participants in the DoD-wide civilian personnel files maintained by DoD. However, individual DoD agencies often retain information on who has participated in such programs in agency-level personnel data systems. Based on what is available from those agencies that track such information, we know that participation was high through the mid-1980s, declined dramatically in the late 1980s and early 1990s, and has been increasing in recent years.

Pre-Employment Internships Exist in DoD but Are Not Common

Although DoD runs pre-employment intern programs of the three types we have discussed, structured, centralized summer intern programs like those found in the corporate world are relatively rare in DoD. Indeed, Oldman and Hamadeh's *Internship Bible* (2002), which lists hundreds of pre-employment internship opportunities, contained only one reference to a DoD pre-employment intern program: a program for law students sponsored by the Office of the General Counsel.

More common are various types of decentralized internships sponsored and coordinated by local managers, although these tend to be less visible than the highly structured and centralized ECPD programs. DoD's pre-employment internships are not explicitly linked to ECPD programs or to general agency hiring goals, nor do these programs receive high-level visibility. The use of co-op programs primarily focuses on engineering and computer science students, as is the case in the private sector.

Because ECPD program participants are hired into permanent career-conditional positions through a variety of hiring authorities, it is not possible to obtain centralized information on the number of ECPD program participants. Managers of the various programs do track the number of participants from year to year, however (detailed information about specific programs is in Appendix A). We found that the size of ECPD programs that have existed for 10 years or more peaked in the mid- to late 1980s and then declined until the late 1990s, when interest in such programs started to increase again. In addition, several agencies recently created or are creating new ECPD programs to meet anticipated personnel needs.

As indicated by Figure 2.3, the number of pre-employment interns (identified in the data as *student trainees*) in DoD has increased since FY 1998, although the numbers are still rather small (just over 3,076 in 2002). The number of student trainees is less than 5 percent of the total number of new hires in DoD and an even smaller percentage of the number of accessions (which includes transfers and returns to duty).[14] A vast majority of these student trainees are GS-3 through GS-5.

---

[14] In FY 2001, there were 96,060 DoD accessions, of which 70,168 were new hires. This is up from FY 2000, when there were 94,329 accessions and 68,511 new hires. See U.S. Office of Personnel Management, Federal Civilian Workforce Statistics Employment and Trends, January 1999 to January 2000 (http://www.opm.gov/feddata/html/empt.asp).

Figure 2.3
Number of DoD Student Trainees, by Fiscal Year

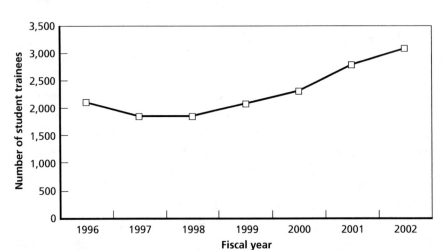

SOURCE: FORMIS (DMDC).

RAND MG138-2.3

DoD Uses Two Federal Programs for Hiring Student Employees

In the federal government, pre-employment interns of all types are hired through one of two programs within the Student Educational Employment Program (SEEP). The Student Temporary Employment Program (STEP) is an option for agencies that want to hire students on a part-time or short-term basis to get work done. The Student Career Experience Program (SCEP) is oriented more toward training and development and is designed to groom students for permanent positions. Eligibility in the latter program is limited to students enrolled at least half time in an educational program, but this is fairly generously defined and includes everything from people pursuing a GED (general equivalency diploma) to Ph.D. candidates.

The main difference between STEP and SCEP is that STEP allows agencies to hire students into any job that needs to be done. Agencies hiring through SCEP must provide work experience related to the student's educational program and career goals. SCEP requires that the agency, student, and school agree in writing about the nature of work assignments, the schedule of work assignments and class attendance, evaluation procedures, and requirements for continuation and successful completion.

Additional information about the organization of these two programs is in Chapter Four.

Number of Pre-Employment Interns Varies According to Occupational Area and Service

DoD pre-employment interns (student trainees) can be found in many different occupational areas, but a large proportion are in the scientific, technical, and business areas. As Figure 2.4 shows, 39 percent of trainees are classified in the engineering and architecture field, with an additional 15 percent in general or mathematical science. Business and industry and accounting claim another 14 percent of student trainees, and 16 percent are in administration and office support. (It is likely that many of the student trainees in this last category

Figure 2.4
Occupational Areas of DoD Student Trainees, FY 2002

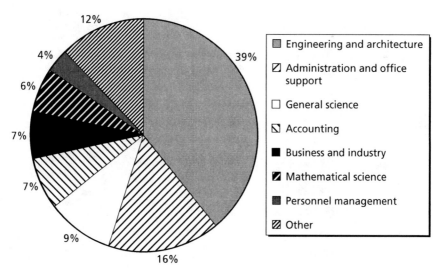

SOURCE: FORMIS (DMDC).
RAND MG138-2.4

are participating in STEP rather than the more career-oriented SCEP.)

Figure 2.5 shows the breakdown of DoD pre-employment interns (again, student trainees) by service and agency. As can be seen, the Army employs nearly half of all DoD student trainees; the Navy employs 30 percent; the Air Force, 15 percent. Between FY 1997 and FY 2002, the number of trainees increased by 150 percent in the Air Force, 81 percent in the Army, and 20 percent in the Navy. Within the Army, the largest employer by far is the Army Corps of Engineers; in the Air Force, the largest employer is the Air Force Materiel Command (AFMC).

Among other DoD agencies, the Defense Information Systems Agency (DISA), DFAS, the Defense Logistics Agency (DLA), and DCMA are the largest employers of student trainees. DFAS and DCMA in particular have increased their numbers of trainees in recent years.

Figure 2.5
Number of DoD Student Trainees, by Service and Agency, FY 2002

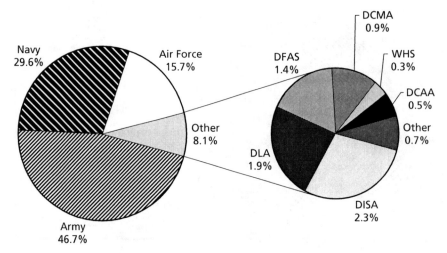

SOURCE: FORMIS (DMDC).
RAND MG138-2.5

Between December 1998 and January 2002, the new DoD hires[15] were distributed as follows across the major departments: Army, 33 percent; Navy, 22 percent; Air Force, 33 percent; DLA, 2 percent; and other DoD, 12 percent.[16] Thus, it appears that relative to the number of new hires, the Army and Navy have more student trainees and the Air Force has fewer.

This review of DoD's use of internships suggests that the range of available options is wide and includes programs that can be used to hire pre-employment interns.

Lessons for DoD

DoD's use of internships tends to be quite different from that of private corporations. Whereas DoD uses more ECPD programs than the private sector does, private corporations favor summer intern programs—a type of pre-employment internship rarely used in DoD. Is there anything DoD can learn from the private sector's use of pre-employment internships?

Compared to the other two types of pre-employment intern programs—part-time internships and co-op programs—summer internships offer three distinct advantages. First, they give corporations access to the broadest pool of candidates. Unlike part-time interns, who need to work somewhere near their school, and co-op participants, who must attend a school that supports co-op experiences, almost any student at any school is a potential candidate for a summer internship. Summer internships also fit in well with the traditional academic schedule, and most students are willing to relocate for a paid (and sometimes even for an unpaid) summer internship. Second, summer internships allow students to explore a variety of career options in that students can choose to be a summer intern at different

---

[15] This look at new hires excludes transfers and returns to duty.

[16] Calculations are based on U.S. Office of Personnel Management, Federal Civilian Workforce Statistics Employment and Trends, January 1999 to January 2002 (http://www.opm.gov/feddata/html/empt.asp).

organizations in different summers. Co-op and part-time internships, in contrast, require a student to make a greater level of commitment to an organization. Third, summer internships are usually open to students in a wide range of disciplines, whereas co-op programs tend to focus in the science and engineering areas.

One key advantage of a centralized summer intern program is that it allows managers to compare and rank intern program partici-pants and make hiring decisions accordingly. The screening role is a crucial one for most pre-employment intern programs. It is just as valuable to learn that someone is not a good fit (and to avoid hiring him or her) as it is to learn that someone is a good fit (and to hire that person). Although some organizations had the goal of acquiring all new hires from their pool of interns, not one of them had the goal of hiring all its pre-employment interns. The screening role is thus critical for selecting employees with the greatest potential.

The many benefits of pre-employment internships found in the private sector may suggest that DoD should consider expanding its use of these programs. To evaluate its options fully, however, DoD needs to consider whether a change in its mix of programs would be appropriate for its specific recruiting objectives and organizational culture.

In addressing this issue, it is important to consider the practices successful organizations use for intern programs, as well as the organi-zational options they use to structure such programs—both of which are important in determining the success of the programs in serving larger recruiting goals. We explore these issues in the following two chapters. Chapter Three looks at practices that successful organiza-tions use for internships and considers the extent to which DoD might consider adopting or expanding its use of such practices. Chap-ter Four takes a detailed look at how the structure of intern programs can influence the programs' abilities to meet their recruiting goals.

Characteristics of Successful Intern Programs

There is an extensive body of literature on guidelines, or best practices, for pre-employment internships, but there is no similar body of literature for ECPD programs. In this chapter, we identify those features of successful pre-employment internships that have been emphasized in the literature. We then discuss how some of these practices apply to ECPD programs and consider the implications for DoD more broadly.

If the primary purpose of intern programs is to screen and recruit individuals for permanent positions, then, to be successful, such programs need to attract desirable student candidates and generate interest in the organization during the internships. What qualities or skills constitute "desirable" will vary from organization to organization. Once students become interns, however, it is important to manage them effectively, both to their benefit and to that of the organization. Such considerations are also important for ECPD programs, with an additional consideration—that of ensuring that program participants progress appropriately in moving into more-advanced positions.

Characteristics of Successful Pre-Employment Internships

A theme running through all the information on successful pre-employment intern programs is to do them well or not at all. These programs can be costly to run, not only in terms of explicit dollar amounts, but also in terms of the management attention required to mentor and evaluate program participants. A program that is not well run can create a negative reputation for the employer—a reputation that can go beyond the individual who had a bad intern experience. If the programs are well managed—in other words, if their success relative to articulated organizational goals is monitored, program changes are made as needed, and a close link to permanent hiring is maintained—the payoff can be high. But if the programs are not integrated with permanent hiring and are viewed primarily as temporary employment programs or a way to get work done while regular employees are on vacation, then the potential benefits are much lower.

The characteristics of successful pre-employment internships can be effectively discussed in terms of recruitment and selection of participants, and management of interns during the program.

Recruitment and Selection of Participants

As noted in the introduction to this chapter, successful intern programs need to attract desirable students and generate interest in the job during the students' internships. The literature provides several guidelines for recruiting and selecting participants for internships.

Carefully consider the organization's needs to ensure that potential candidates are a good fit. The existing literature on pre-employment internships encourages careful selection of interns: "Students you hire for intern and co-op opportunities should be as carefully chosen as permanent employees" (Patterson, 1997). Careful selection in accordance with the organization's goals is important for two reasons in particular. First, if an organization's goal is to recruit permanent employees, it does not want an intern it would not consider for a permanent position. Second, because even an unpaid internship is expensive in terms of employee time, resources, and support, it makes no sense to waste an internship on an unworthy person.

To attract desirable students, know what students are looking for. In a recent survey of graduating seniors (Scott Resource Group, 1999), students ranked their reasons for choosing the pre-employment internships they had participated in. Ranked first was "job content," followed by "will look impressive on my resume," "relevance to my degree," and "to learn about the field and or company." Effective intern programs benefit both the participants and the organizations they serve. While organizations need to understand their own goals for using an intern program, they also need to know what potential participants expect to gain.

Identify ways to gain access to potential participants. Students typically learn about potential internships in a variety of ways. The Scott Resource Group study (1999) found that students like to read about programs on the Web, but also like to attend a campus presentation or job fair booth, where they can ask questions and talk to a "real person." These student preferences suggest the importance of providing both information that students can access freely at their convenience (e.g., through a Website) and opportunities for one-to-one contact between students and the organization. Students are interested in learning about particular job or career areas. Increasingly, students expect to know what they will be working on before they sign on.

To obtain good candidates, firms employ various recruiting methods. According to Brooks and Greene (1998), for-profit companies rank career fairs and on-campus recruiting as their most effective recruitment methods. The same study shows that nonprofits (including government) report "listing with career service" and listing in "national internship guides" as their top two approaches. In light of the student preferences for one-on-one contact discussed above, the methods preferred by the surveyed nonprofits may not be optimal. Government agencies may need to consider another route to attracting students to internships: supplementing their Web-based and other job postings with campus recruiting or similar avenues that offer an opportunity for direct contact.

All the firms and DoD agencies we spoke with use some form of Web-based application process. Recruiters encourage potential candidates to fill out a Web application. HP's system, which uses Recruitsoft software, is particularly innovative. It allows the recruiter who spoke with and encouraged a candidate to apply to attach an evaluation of that candidate to his or her Web application. This evaluation can be seen on HP's intranet, thus serving as an aid to those who make the hiring decisions.

Management of Interns During the Program

Once interns have been successfully recruited, it is critically important that their internships are managed effectively so that the program's goals will be met. In our review of the literature, we found numerous proffered best practices for managing pre-employment intern programs (sources include Gold, 2002; Scott Resource Group, 1999; and Cunningham, 2002). We have grouped these practices under five guidelines, as follows:

Select good mentors and job assignments. Supervision, mentorship, and the match between individual and task were all mentioned repeatedly. Good mentorship is advocated as the best way to guide a student's development. Work in the literature on best practices suggests that supervision and mentorship of interns is key (Patterson, 1997) and that careful selection and training of supervisors and mentors is imperative (Cunningham, 2002).

Mentorship has several benefits from a corporate perspective. First, interns who have a positive experience are more likely to be interested in a permanent position. Second, engaged mentors and supervisors are more likely to have the ability to make an effective assessment of the intern. Third, interns who have a positive experience are likely to view the firm and the profession positively and to report that positive reputation back to their university, both formally and informally. Finally, a good internship experience is more likely to be a productive internship experience, in terms of getting work done.

One author (Watson, 1995) notes that there is a difference between supervision and mentorship, and some benefits might accrue from dividing these roles among different persons: "Another unique aspect of Union Carbide's program is a clear, almost church-and-state demarcation between mentoring and supervision." There are several reasons for doing this: "Like most employees, interns will more openly discuss concerns with someone who is not a supervisor. Some supervisors, on the other hand, may shy away from certain mentoring responsibilities because they fear breaching managerial protocol."

Provide students with interesting work. Providing students with meaningful work experiences, giving students one or more real projects to complete, and providing students with experience in numerous aspects of the company's activities—all of these receive attention in lists of best practices. Interns do not want to do only "busywork"; they want to feel that they are contributing and getting a real sense of what goes on in the company and what it is like to work there.

Provide benefits. Even an unpaid internship can be appealing if there are tangible benefits. Assistance with relocation or housing, transportation, etc., can contribute to a positive internship experience. Social events, such as an orientation or organized outings or gatherings, can also embellish an internship.

Administer the program carefully. We found numerous pieces of administrative advice for successful internships. Pre-employment intern programs are encouraged to maintain support from the highest levels in the company (e.g., the CEO) and to regularly engage and communicate with individuals within the organization who have an interest in or provide resources to support the program. Ongoing engagement with these interested parties is important for ensuring that program awareness is high, program objectives are being met, and areas for improvement are identified. Program administrators should be encouraged to respond to problems quickly; if a poor match of personalities or a difference in expectations is identified and addressed early, the intern may still have a positive experience.

Since reputation is paramount, it is important to ensure that even interns who will not receive offers of permanent employment have a positive experience. Several sources suggest that programs provide an intern handbook or Website of information so that interns can consult resources without having to turn to a supervisor or mentor, thus increasing their feelings of self-reliance and empowerment.

Be recruitment-minded throughout the program. If the main goal of a pre-employment intern program is recruitment, then programs should be run in a recruitment-minded way. In some respects, this guideline incorporates all the characteristics discussed in this chapter. Being recruitment-minded starts with careful selection of candidates and extends to thoughtful monitoring and evaluation of each student's progress as an intern. Then, at the end of the internship, it should be reasonably clear whether the student will make a good employee.

Organizations can take the internship as an opportunity to inform students of the benefits of working for them. One DFAS manager mentioned that DFAS emphasizes the 40-hour workweek, as opposed to the workweeks of 60+ hours typical at major accounting firms. This is similar to the Internal Revenue Service's emphasis on "time for fun, friends and family" on its recruiting Website.[1] Benefits and job security are other key selling points.

An organization's chances of hiring an intern are maximized if it offers permanent employment in a timely fashion relative to the end of the intern's participation in the program. Some programs make employment offers even before the internship is officially over.

Case Study Example: Ford Motor Company
Ford Motor Company devotes substantial attention to its summer intern program, following many of the practices mentioned above and reaping the benefits in terms of solid conversion rates of employees to new hires. The summer intern program at Ford is clearly and explicitly a means of screening and hiring entry-level employees who will then participate in Ford's ECPD program. Summer interns are carefully screened, going through an application and interview process that closely mirrors the one Ford uses for permanent employees. Nearly all interns come to work during the summer and work in the Ford headquarters office in Dearborn, Michigan. Over the course of the summer, interns are rated by their managers on a common set of metrics related to leadership potential. By the end of the summer, each operational unit has determined its hiring requirements for the following year and is able to make offers of permanent employment to some number of the most highly ranked summer interns before they return to school.

---

[1] See http://www.jobs.irs.gov.

Approximately 80 percent of Ford's summer interns get an employment offer, and, of those, about 75 percent accept. Program managers would like to know why those candidates who decline Ford's offers do so, but they find it difficult to get useful responses from them. Most will not tell where they are going; others provide a general response, such as, "I accepted another job because it offered more opportunity." What a manager really wants to know is why it seemed like a better opportunity.

In addition to summer interns, Ford has about 100 to 200 co-op participants. Currently, the co-op programs are not centrally aligned and are driven primarily by local managers. Ford looks at co-op positions, which are more like real jobs than internships are, as an opportunity to evaluate a person's fit for a permanent position while getting real work done. Ford is considering whether a greater degree of central alignment would be beneficial for the co-op program.

Ford does not gather as much data on co-op participants as it does on interns, but it estimates that 65 to 70 percent of co-op participants receive a permanent job offer and that their acceptance rate is higher than that of interns.

Case Study Example: CIA
The CIA offers several pre-employment intern programs. Unlike some organizations, the CIA does not make a clear distinction between summer interns, part-time interns, and co-op participants. Each type of intern makes the same level of commitment to the agency and thus goes through a similar selection process.

The CIA takes the selection process very seriously. Student employees go through a screening process equally as rigorous as the one permanent employees go through. Just like regular employees, they are subjected to health screening, background checks, polygraph tests, etc. This process is very time-consuming and costly, which is why the CIA makes the up-front investment in rigorous initial screening.

The CIA also sponsors traditional programs that include the full range of pre-employment internships. The agency does not distinguish among the different types of pre-employment interns in tracking such information as hiring rates and conversion rates, however. To the agency, they are all student employees, and the different programs just help the agency attract a wider pool of students.

The CIA's Student Trainee, or co-op, program allows students to alternate school and work and is only for students enrolled in schools that support co-op programs. Otherwise, it is the same as the CIA's Internship Program, which requires participants to commit upfront to two tours with the CIA. Each tour lasts 90 days (three months), although the CIA has been somewhat flexible about tour length. Both tours can be in the summer, or students can do one tour in the summer and one during the school year (perhaps delaying their graduation). The CIA requires students to commit for such a long period because it wants to make its up-front investment in interns' in-depth pre-employment screening worthwhile.

Two additional intern programs, both for the Directorate of Operations (DO), were started in the past few years: the DO Undergraduate Student Intern Program and the DO Graduate Student Intern Program. Both are six months long—either January to June or July to December. The DO formerly did not hire pre-employment interns, because of its requirements for screening and for longer tours. But it has now set up its own program, with different requirements, which is run through the recruiting center.

Responsibility for mentoring, developing the training program, evaluating the interns, etc., is decentralized to the individual operating units within the CIA. There is no centralized mentoring guide, although the recruiting center is considering whether to develop one, given that it is recognized as an effective practice. A few managers in one of the operating units, the Directorate of Intelligence, have prepared a seminar for student mentors, and other managers have found it to be very useful.

Hiring is a key objective of the summer program, and about 85 percent of interns are hired on as permanent employees. The other 15 percent are primarily interns who decline permanent offers of employment, usually because they have decided that the CIA is not for them and that they want to pursue other career options. Because of the intense screening that the CIA does for student positions, it is rare for students to fail in the internship and not get a permanent offer.

Implications for ECPD Programs

There is no distinct literature providing guidance on the characteristics of effective ECPD programs. We were, however, able to draw some useful observations about such characteristics from our case studies and Internet review.

ECPD programs are not a substitute for pre-employment internships. Although several DoD components have ECPD programs that are not linked to pre-employment intern programs, we observed several organizations—for instance, Ford, Cigna, the CIA, and DFAS—whose highly structured pre-employment intern programs serve as recruiting tools for formal ECPD programs. In these cases, the organizations appear to use the pre-employment intern programs as a screening tool precisely because the ECPD program is a substantial commitment on the part of the organization to the training and development of a new hire.

Even though ECPD programs focus less than pre-employment intern programs on recruitment because the participant is a bona fide employee rather than a potential hire, quality mentoring and rotational assignments are nonetheless especially important parts of ECPD programs. The objective of ECPD programs is to provide the support and development that leads to long, successful careers with the organization. Thus, the most successful programs are those designed with these long-term objectives in mind.

DoD ECPD programs appear to be at least as well organized as ECPD programs in the private sector. They are generally tied to some type of workforce planning effort or needs assessment that projects the need for personnel in certain skilled positions in three to five years. Analyses conducted by the Army and the Air Force suggest that their intern programs have been successful over time in the sense that ECPD program graduates, when compared to individuals who were hired into local trainee positions or who were hired directly into journeyman-level positions, have higher retention rates and are promoted more quickly into management positions.

Of course, high retention rates for ECPD program graduates are a useful measure of success only if those hired into the program are all desirable as employees. Our interviews with ECPD program managers in DoD generated mixed perspectives on this issue. Some of the program managers were still making aggressive use of the Outstanding Scholars hiring authority and attributed much of the ECPD program's success to the desirability of candidates hired under that authority. Other program managers offered a similar perspective on the Federal Career Intern hiring authority. Still other program mangers were restricting their use of the Outstanding Scholars authority but claimed to be making aggressive use of the probationary period to get rid of new ECPD program hires who were not working out.

Both DoD and private-sector organizations emphasize structured training and development and rotational assignments for ECPD programs designed to create broad, upwardly mobile future leaders. In private-sector organizations, these programs have an implicit mobility requirement: Candidates who want to remain employed by the organization must be willing to go where the job opportunities are. In DoD, ECPD programs typically have an explicit mobility requirement: Participants must declare their willingness to move. DoD ECPD program managers did, however, report that participants commonly refuse to move, and that the program rarely invokes the mobility requirement. Instead, the managers work with the person to identify a local placement rather than lose the person or force him or her to move.

Lessons for DoD

A common theme running through the practices offered in this chapter is the importance of keeping organizational goals in mind when designing and administering an intern program, whether of the pre-employment or the ECPD kind. A clear understanding of program goals is especially critical in selecting participants for the programs and in evaluating their work as interns to determine whether to make an offer of full employment (in pre-employment programs) or to keep employees on track for advancement (in ECPD programs). DoD can clearly benefit from applying these ideas in its internship programs.

A key reason why private corporations are able to benefit from pre-employment intern programs is the amount of effort they put into evaluating program participants and the fact that they offer employment to the most successful participants. Since recruiting is a primary goal of pre-employment intern programs, companies typically use substantial care in "selling" a student on the organization during the internship. The first, and perhaps most important, way to do this is to get students excited about the work that goes on in the organization and the available career opportunities. Several organizations we interviewed, including some within DoD, emphasized the importance of three elements: ensuring that intern-program mentors are top employees who are enthusiastic about their jobs, providing students with an opportunity to contribute to a real project that means something to the company, and providing students with an opportunity to learn about the variety of things that go on in the organization.

It is essential to keep in mind, however, that there are costs entailed in running an effective intern program. Pre-employment internships require a considerable investment of time and other resources, a point clearly taken into account by organizations in deciding whether to use such a program or in selecting the kind of program to use. The nature of the work an organization performs appears to influence the efficiency of using pre-employment internships as a screening tool. Both the CIA and Northrop Grumman face a special challenge in that detailed (and costly) background checks and security clearances are necessary for most, if not all, positions, including pre-employment internships. The fact that such detailed screening must be done up-front reduces the value of screening that might go on during the internship. At the CIA, this cost-benefit calculus has led to both a requirement that pre-employment intern candidates commit to two internship periods (approximately six months total) and an emphasis on hiring as many pre-employment interns as possible. At Northrop Grumman, this calculus has led to a preference for co-op programs over summer or part-time internships.

While it is important to monitor closely the processes through which individuals are recruited for internships and subsequently selected for permanent employment or career advancement, it is equally important to ensure that programs are designed to help participants fulfill program objectives. Mentoring and supervision are important for supporting these objectives.

In addition, it should be noted that in regard to many aspects of internships, there is no one "best practice" appropriate for all organizations. For example, different recruitment methods (e.g., Website listings, career fairs) are effective for different candidates for different positions. To the extent possible, it may be useful to use a variety of methods, so as to reach different potential participants and to allow for considerable flexibility in selecting among available approaches.

Importantly, the success of an internship program depends not only on the practices used, but also on the way the program is structured. Issues such as who funds a program, who does the recruiting and hiring, who evaluates interns, etc., can greatly influence whether a program achieves its goals. Organizational options for pre-employment internships and ECPD programs are the subject of the next chapter.

CHAPTER FOUR

Organizational Options for Pre-Employment Intern Programs and Early Career Professional Development Programs

This chapter discusses the ways in which both pre-employment internships and ECPD programs are organized, the goal being to better understand how program organization influences program success. DoD can then use this information to identify and adopt as appropriate those organizational practices that are optimal for its recruiting and training needs.

The two broad categories of intern programs—pre-employment and ECPD—include similar sets of core activities and share a range of organizational options. In examining both types of intern programs, we focus on six core activities: funding, recruiting, selecting participants, mentoring participants and developing programs, evaluating programs and participants, and facilitating participant migration to permanent (pre-employment interns) or full-performance (ECPD interns) positions. We use our case study data to provide examples of how different programs are organized. Our analysis considers the implications of various organizational options and describes the characteristics associated with successful programs to the extent that they have become clear to us.

In discussing the organizational options used in both public and private organizations, we also pay special attention to the ways in which DoD differs from other organizations because of federal civil service hiring processes or other rules affecting DoD internships.

Organizational options necessarily include questions of centralization and decentralization. In complex organizations such as those considered for this research, decentralization can take many forms.

Organizations may decide to carve themselves up in different ways and to attach different labels to their organizational levels. For simplicity, we employ a generic terminology and focus on some basic forms of decentralization. An organization (e.g., a corporation, DoD) may be divided into some number of subunits (e.g., corporate divisions, DoD services and agencies), and these subunits may be further divided (and so on). We use the term *operational unit* to refer to a distinct subunit of an organization, one having specific roles, responsibilities, and objectives that contribute to the goals of the organization as a whole, and which may be embedded in a hierarchy of organizational subunits. We think of operational units as the places where the real work of the organization gets done.

In addition to having this hierarchical organizational structure (and the rather straightforward decentralization decisions that may flow from it), large organizations often recognize the importance of functional or occupationally based groups or communities. For example, a large organization may have a need for accountants or contracting specialists that cuts across many of its operational units. And it may, as a result, see a value in coordinating the hiring and the career progression of this identifiable set of individuals. We use the term *functional community* to describe these cross-cutting groups of employees who work in related occupational areas. It is important to recognize that members of a functional community typically will also be associated with a particular operational unit.[1]

Organizational Options for Pre-Employment Intern Programs

As noted above, in examining our pre-employment intern programs, we focused on six core activities: funding, recruiting, selecting par-

---

[1] In some organizations, hierarchical organizational subunits are called *functional units* because they are defined by the organizational subunits' primary function or responsibility. We call these divisions *subunits* to distinguish them from functional communities, as described in this paragraph.

ticipants, mentoring participants and developing programs, evaluating programs and participants, and facilitating participant migration to permanent employment. We discuss these activities next, describing how each one is structured in different settings for pre-employment intern programs.

Funding

The different ways in which programs are funded have important implications for how managers at different levels perceive the programs and how involved managers are in different stages of the programs. The key issue concerns who provides resources such as personnel authorizations[2] and dollars for intern salaries, training program development, program management, recruiting, travel, and training. Funding for pre-employment intern programs can be either local or centralized in a variety of ways (e.g., organizationwide, subunitwide, functionwide).

Within DoD, the use of co-ops and part-time internships is generally not centralized at the service level, although the Air Force has initiated a centrally funded service-level program for 250 student trainee positions for FY 2003. The plan is to increase that number to 500 by FY 2007.[3] More common are co-op programs initiated and coordinated at the local level. For example, Robins Air Force Base has developed a co-op program in conjunction with several local technical colleges.[4] However, even though our case studies allow us to understand how some internship programs are funded, there is no centralized source of information that allows us to document the variety of such programs in DoD.

---

[2] DoD organizations face constraints on both the number of people they can hire and the amount of money they can spend. To hire a new employee, an organization must have a personnel authorization and ensure that it is funded. Authorizations allocated to individual units are a way for DoD to ensure that total civilian end-strength does not exceed congressional limits.

[3] See http://www.afmc.wpafb.af.mil/HQ-AFMC/PA/news/archive/2002/mar/HQ_Coop students.htm.

[4] See http://www.afmc.wpafb.af.mil/HQ-AFMC/PA/news/archive/2001/aug/Robins_Coop program.htm.

Funding is sometimes split between local and more-centralized functions. For example, funding for DCAA's pre-employment intern program is centralized at DCAA's regional budget level. Without shouldering any formal costs, managers of local operating units get the chance to evaluate and train candidates, the only cost to the local office being the time spent mentoring and training interns. At HP, however, the cost (salary, training) of interns is borne by the local operating unit, although the cost of recruiting, along with some other administrative aspects of the program, is borne by the company as a whole. At Ford, organizational subunits (which are defined by function) primarily bear the costs of pre-employment intern programs. The subunits must cover the employment cost of the individual and assign mentor(s) to each program participant. Functional communities also cover administrative costs. Thus, operational managers do not incur any direct costs for interns.

Recruiting

As discussed in the previous chapter, the methods used to recruit and select interns are important to program success. Similarly, the way in which recruitment and selection efforts are structured affects the outcomes of these processes. All of the agencies and firms included in our case studies centralize their recruiting for pre-employment internships to some extent; nonetheless, there are important differences in how recruiting is organized.

One difference stems from program size and scope. At DCAA, the small size of the program and its focus on a few functional communities make recruiting easier. DCAA regional staff have developed relationships with the relevant personnel at local colleges and universities, and they rely on these informal relationships to find candidates to recruit. The functional focus of the program makes it easy to let students know exactly what their duties will be, which is attractive to students. Larger organizations recruiting for a wider range of occupational areas tend to structure their recruiting efforts in much more formal ways. For example, the centralization of intern recruiting at Ford limits duplication of effort. HR personnel at Ford coordinate the recruiting activities of about 900 line managers who have the additional responsibility of campus recruiting. These line managers go to campuses to do interviews, give briefings to groups, etc., and they direct interested students to the Web application process. At that point, HR takes over, controlling the number of invitations that are offered based on information on needs from organizational subunits and a model of hiring proportions.

At HP, the process is a bit more decentralized. While the operational managers at HP pay the salaries of their interns, the costs of recruiting and monitoring them are funded centrally through HR. HP has an extensive recruiting network, including HR recruiters who have strong relationships with specific universities, and volunteer recruiters who are drawn from staff alumni. Because of this reliance on volunteers, HP's recruiting is less formal than Ford's. The volunteers have more control of the timing and pace of their contribution to the recruiting effort, and centralized (corporatewide) HR monitors their efforts.

All three of the organizations just discussed rely on college recruiting as an important aspect of their recruiting efforts. DCAA has informal contacts with local schools; Ford and HP have more-formal college relations—they maintain relationships with, respectively, about 50 and 47 colleges nationwide. At both Ford and HP, each school is the responsibility of one person (an executive at Ford, and a staffer from the college staffing office at HP) who is in charge of managing the relationship with that school. These liaisons oversee recruitment at the school, public affairs, research and development, and college relations. Through their liaisons, these companies support research activities at the schools, have relationships with faculty, and coordinate on-campus recruiting.

Selecting Participants

As with funding, the selection of interns from the applicant pool can be either centralized or local. Central hiring is more likely than central funding to cause tension with local managers, however: Local managers are generally happy to have a "free" intern paid for out of a higher-level budget, but they are less likely to employ someone in their office whom they had no part in selecting.

At Ford, hiring is centralized. Once students have been recruited and have applied for a position, HR uses the interview information and the online assessment tool to decide which ones to invite to Ford's "leadership conference." HR controls the number of invitations that are offered. Operations tells HR how many it needs to hire; HR then invites a certain number that should result in that many hires based on a model.

At HP, the initial screening and evaluation are centralized, and functional managers make the hiring decisions. Operational managers have the final authority, but they only see candidates who pass the initial central screening. In our private-sector examples, hiring authority follows funding: Ford's pre-employment internships are centrally funded and centrally hired; HP's intern positions come out of local budgets, and local operational managers make the hiring decisions.

Hiring Authorities for Pre-Employment Internship in DoD

DoD's hiring practices with regard to pre-employment interns merit special note in this discussion. In selecting participants for pre-employment internships, DoD organizations must follow federal hiring rules designed to protect the merit-based hiring system. This implies that DoD managers may not have the level of flexibility enjoyed by their private-sector counterparts. Nevertheless, special hiring authorities are available for managers who wish to hire students for pre-employment intern programs. Students can be hired as "excepted service" employees through the Student Educational Employment Program (SEEP). As part of the excepted service, candidates under SEEP are exempt from the competitive service regulations. Established in 1994, SEEP now consists of two programs: the Student Temporary Employment Program (STEP) and the Student Career Experience Program (SCEP).[5] These programs give students and

---

[5] The authority for these programs is in Schedule B 213.3202(a) and (b). These two programs resulted from the consolidation of four prior programs: the cooperative education program, the federal junior fellowship program, the stay-in-school program, and the Harry S. Truman scholarship program.

agencies more flexibility than the standard competitive civil service hiring authorities do. SEEP authority may be used at many organizational levels. Our interviews suggest that local DoD managers are interested in the programs but afraid of running afoul of the rules and seek guidance from their commands on how to use the hiring authority.[6]

There are significant differences between STEP and SCEP. As noted in Chapter Two, STEP allows agencies to hire students into any job that needs to be done, whereas agencies hiring through SCEP must provide work experience related to the student's educational program and career goals. Another crucial difference between the programs is that SCEP students can directly convert to permanent competitive service positions without going through the formal, competitive hiring process. (This noncompetitive conversion process is less stringent than the formal hiring process, but it nonetheless has specific requirements, including 640 hours of service under SCEP,[7] completion of academic program, and recommendation by the employing agency.) Such conversions are not possible directly from STEP, although students can move from STEP to SCEP, and some of their hours of service may count toward the 640-hour requirement for noncompetitive conversion. Also noteworthy is that SCEP alumni can noncompetitively convert to permanent positions in any federal agency, not just the one in which they did their SCEP, as long as they do so within 120 days of program completion.

DoD agencies may also use the normal temporary hiring authority to hire pre-employment interns. For example, DCAA has used the normal temporary hiring authority to bring in students just for the summer (this program is, however, not particularly active now). DCAA uses SCEP to hire college students that it intends to eventually recruit, and it uses STEP to hire office help. DCAA's hiring is done centrally by regional HR (again, hiring of interns occurs at the same level as the funding).

---

[6] See http://www.opm.gov/employ/students/2133202.htm.

[7] These 640 hours must be completed while the individual is still a student.

This brief review of DoD hiring authorities for pre-employment intern programs suggests that DoD organizations do have means of bringing in pre-employment interns and, in fact, encourage DoD to adopt the kinds of structured, training-oriented programs found in successful private-sector organizations. However, the rules governing these programs can make the process of recruiting and selecting interns resource intensive. Moreover, as we discuss later in this chapter, additional restrictions govern whether a pre-employment intern can be hired as a permanent employee.

Mentoring Participants and Developing Programs

As described in our discussion of effective practices, mentoring and supervision are two critical components of a successful intern program. However, mentoring and supervisory responsibilities can be variously distributed—sometimes the two roles are one person's responsibility; other times, a distinction (sometimes formal, but typically not) is made between the supervisor and mentor. At DCAA, for example, mentorship and training content are informal and are left to the discretion of the operational managers.

At Ford, all organizational subunits assign mentors to intern program participants to guide them in selecting professional development assignments. Operational managers have the primary responsibility for mentoring and training-program development, but do receive some central support, in the form of such items as development of training materials for mentors. In addition, Ford has set up a buddy system whereby summer interns are matched with new employees who can provide them with advice on more-informal issues, such as what is fun to do in the local area. DFAS has a similar system that distinguishes supervisors from mentors and buddies.

At HP, mentorship and training are the responsibility of the operational managers, within some centralized guidelines. HP has a very strong mentorship system, not because the company offers formal mentorship training (they do not), but because its corporate and recruiting culture creates opportunities for students to have numerous informal mentors. In addition to the formal mentors assigned to students by the operational managers, HR recruiters assigned to a school often serve as informal mentors with the intent of maintaining a relationship with the students and encouraging them to return as interns for multiple years and ultimately to take permanent positions. Volunteer alumni recruiters also serve as informal mentors, even when students end up in different operational areas.

Evaluating Programs and Participants

To know whether a program is meeting its goals, it must be evaluated. To determine whether pre-employment interns are worth hiring as permanent staff, they must be evaluated. The range of possible ways to organize the evaluation activities runs from formal to informal and includes variation in terms of who does the evaluating.

Once students are in the Ford summer intern program, the evaluation process is highly structured. Each intern is evaluated on the same basis with an instrument that is developed centrally. The evaluation instrument is very detailed and is based on the "Ford leadership behaviors." Candidates are rated on a scale of 1 to 10, and the meaning of each number is described in great detail in the instrument (e.g., what behavior would be evidence of level 9 performance). At Ford, program evaluation appears to be centralized, currently focusing on cost-benefit analysis. In contrast, DCAA's program and interns are evaluated in a largely informal way, by word of mouth. That said, DCAA reports that the program is well regarded by students and college counselors within the region, and approximately 60 percent of interns convert to permanent employment.

At HP, interns are formally evaluated by their managers, and the evaluations are recorded and subsequently used to inform final hiring decisions. Hiring into permanent positions is done in much the same way as the initial intern hires are: Recruitsoft software allows staff to input evaluations. Managers who think an intern is top-notch can hire him or her if they have a "req" (requisition) available, or, if they do not have a req, can let managers who do have an open req know about the candidate.

As mentioned earlier, it is difficult to come up with a good measure of the success of a pre-employment intern program. HP evaluates overall program success based on conversion rate. However, due to ongoing software and reporting issues stemming from a recent merger with Compaq, HP was unable to provide us with their current conversion rate, which will be HP's key program metric as soon as it can be calculated. Indeed, all organizations we interviewed as part of our case studies track conversion rate either formally or informally. However, the discussions made clear that while the conversion rate is a useful piece of information, it is not a metric for which "higher" always means "better." As noted, pre-employment intern programs serve both a recruiting function and a screening function. A program that screens out a poor candidate who may have looked good on paper and interviewed well has been "successful" in some respect, even though that screening implies a lower conversion rate. Another limitation of this measure is that it does not capture how long the organization retains former interns as employees or how successful their careers are relative to the careers of noninterns. Even if these richer measures of "success" were tracked, it is still difficult to determine whether being an intern influences later career opportunities. For example, organizations may have an implicit or explicit policy to more readily promote former interns over noninterns. All of these factors make it hard to objectively evaluate the success of an intern program.

Facilitating Participant Migration to Permanent Employment

If pre-employment internships are ultimately about recruiting, then arranging to hire former interns as permanent employees is arguably the most important part of the process. *Migration* is the term we use to describe the transition as interns graduate from the program (and school) and receive offers for permanent positions.

Migration processes can differ in relation to several factors: the determination of hiring needs, the responsibility for making hiring decisions, and the timing of job offers. We found that both centralized and decentralized approaches to migration can work, although decentralized approaches require more networking initiative on the part of local managers to find a position for a good candidate.

We found a range of options for managing hiring decisions. At Ford, managers make offers to the most promising candidates at the end of the summer intern program. Individual recruiting managers for each organizational subunit know their hiring targets for the next year by August, so they can figure out how many people they want to hire. As a result, managers can respond to intern evaluations as soon as they come in and can have offers ready for the best candidates ("the 8s and 9s") at the end of the summer. Usually, some of the other participants are "deferred"—that is, they do not get an offer before they leave but will get one eventually. At HP, operational managers either hire the best candidates into permanent positions if they have available openings (have the reqs), or try to find other operational managers with open reqs who might want these hires. They do this with support from informal networks and in the context of helpful Recruitsoft software. At DCAA, the HR office monitors degree completion, anticipating students' graduation dates and the opportunity to convert them. If the local manager will not have a position open in the appropriate time frame to hire a good candidate, he or she is often able to "work something out" with a location that will have an opening, thus making sure that DCAA gets the new talent on board.

DoD Interns and Migration to Permanent Employment Status
DoD has little ability to migrate summer program participants to permanent status, which presumably contributes to DoD's limited use of summer programs. Specifically, DoD currently cannot act on the information it would obtain through a summer intern program. There is no mechanism through which DoD can make offers of employment to interns who have completed only one summer program—even when there is an opening in the organization that sponsored the intern.

Although SCEP allows direct conversion to permanent positions, it is of limited use in many cases. SCEP conversion is only possible after 640 hours—16 full-time weeks—of service with a federal agency. Most summer programs are 400 hours, which is only 10 weeks. As a result, a student who spends one successful summer in a DoD internship is not eligible for direct conversion. To become eligible for hiring under SCEP authority, the student would have to either return for a second summer or continue to work part-time during the school year in order to log the additional 6 weeks. Although organizations often try to get successful interns to return for a second summer of internship, it is not always possible or desirable to limit a student's opportunity to explore other options. Indeed, the manager of the summer program for accounting students at DFAS reported that it is valuable for students to get some experience in a private-sector accounting firm.

The ability to make an offer to summer program participants is a significant difference between DoD's organizational options for intern recruiting and those available in the private sector. DoD's inability to make such offers either needs to be compensated for or changed in considering organizational options for DoD pre-employment programs.

Organizational Options for Early Career Professional Development Programs

ECPD programs require essentially the same core activities as pre-employment programs do: funding, recruiting, selecting participants, mentoring participants and developing programs, evaluating programs and participants, and facilitating participant migration to full-performance positions. However, the organizational options for ECPD programs sometimes differ from those of pre-employment programs, often due to the fact that ECPD programs are for permanent employees rather than for students who may—or may not—migrate to permanent employment.

Funding

One distinction between the organization of pre-employment internships and that of ECPD programs relates to funding. While ECPD programs, like pre-employment internships, *can* be funded either locally or centrally, most are centrally funded to some degree. In DoD, many of the activities associated with ECPD are centralized at the service or agency level. Input is often sought from the functional community, but funding is usually centrally provided and a central office directs the other activities as well. As mentioned earlier, this centralization reflects the funding stream and ensuing servicewide goals of the programs.

For DoD ECPD programs, the personnel authorizations used for the program are "centrally owned" so that the specific command or installation where the intern is working does not have to use an authorization to support him or her. In addition, dollars for ECPD program participants, salaries, training program development, program management, recruiting, and travel and training costs often come from centralized budgets. This is not universally true, however. Some agencies (e.g., DFAS) do require operational units to identify authorizations and funding for such programs. In addition, some major commands within services have designed and funded ECPD programs centralized at the command level as a supplement to the centralized programs.

For example, the Army Career Intern Program is centralized (at the service level), and the budget for this program comes directly from the Department of the Army. If local managers do not receive sufficient centrally funded ECPD slots, they may choose to hire additional people with local funds. For these locally hired ECPD program participants, the command or the local installation must pay for all training except for two mandatory centralized classes, which are paid for out of the central budget for every participant, local or central.

In the private sector, ECPD programs tend to be funded similarly to pre-employment intern programs. At Ford, for example, the costs of the ECPD programs are borne primarily by the functional communities as opposed to the local managers. Functional communities must cover the employment cost of the individuals and assign mentor(s) to each program participant.

Recruiting

Recruiting for an ECPD position is, in effect, recruiting for a permanent position with an initial professional development period. As such, recruiting for ECPD generally mirrors recruiting practices for the larger organization, with a few notable exceptions. First, ECPD programs may have their own recruiting staff or organization to supplement or substitute for more-general recruiting elements. Second, recruiting for ECPD focuses on early career candidates with good prospects for development into future professionals in the organization. Third, recruits, in contrast to regular permanent hires, may have to sign mobility agreements or agree to a probationary employment period during the ECPD program.

Recruiting in formal DoD ECPD programs is typically centralized at the organizational level that provides funding. Again, even in highly centralized programs, input from functional communities, operational units, and even local managers may be sought. In DoD, we found that servicewide programs typically recruit through a centralized selection board comprising members of these different communities and organizational subunits.

A range of recruiting practices is found within DoD, however. For example, instead of engaging in explicit recruiting activities, the Army Career Intern Program generally posts its position openings on the USAJOBS Website. Program personnel also have informational brochures and flyers that they make available for the recruiting efforts of others, such as the general-information Army booths at career fairs. Local managers may recruit using their own time and funds. In contrast, the Navy Financial Management Career Center (FMCC) engages in extensive on-campus recruiting in addition to posting job openings in paper and electronic format (both governmental and nongovernmental). The organization tries to build relationships with schools at which it has had success with hires.

When an organization has both pre-employment internships and ECPD programs, one kind of program can be used as a source of recruiting for the other. Ford looks first to the pre-employment intern program as a source of candidates for its FCG ECPD program. If it were possible, Ford would completely fill the ECPD program from the ranks of the intern program. However, some interns decline the permanent offer, and sometimes the skill mix of the interns does not match the organization's hiring needs. Ford's ECPD hiring is similar to its pre-employment intern hiring, with an additional step. Strong candidates are invited to a leadership conference, where they receive additional evaluation before being offered positions in the ECPD program.

Selecting Participants

Participant selection is the process managers go through to decide which applicants will receive traineeship offers and to hire those individuals. Hiring for formal DoD ECPD programs is typically centralized at the organizational level that provides funding, sometimes with input from the functional community or even local managers. A servicewide program will typically recruit and hire through a centralized selection board.

The Army Career Intern Program provides an example of a centralized hiring process that incorporates input from lower levels of the organization in a variety of ways. Each year, commands are asked to specify their intern requirements for the next fiscal year. (There is always more demand than funding for centrally funded interns.) Intern hires are made centrally, but with substantial input from the functional community, operational units, and local managers. Some of the career programs have a centralized board that pulls together representatives from the functional community to make the hiring decisions. However, some career programs, especially in the engineering area, do not use these boards. In career fields for which there are no boards, managers at the local level get to make selections. More generally, central hiring with local input is likely to help resolve some of the "central versus local" tension inherent in the hiring process.

The hiring process is often centrally controlled. In the Navy, the FMCC controls the hiring process centrally. It screens applicants for all positions simultaneously, allowing them to rank their top three locations. The FMCC conducts face-to-face interviews with top candidates, and it sees interviews as extremely important, providing an opportunity to "sell the job" to the applicant. The FMCC then tries to match promising candidates with program openings. At Ford, the recruiting and selection process is similar for both pre-employment interns and ECPD hires. Potential new hires perceive a Ford-wide intern and ECPD program, with centralized funding, recruiting, and hiring.

Hiring Authorities for DoD ECPD Programs

DoD's specific hiring practices with regard to prospective ECPD candidates merit discussion at greater length. Unlike pre-employment interns, who may be appointed to excepted service positions, participants in DoD ECPD programs are typically appointed to full-time, career-conditional positions. As a result, they must go through standard federal government hiring processes. The basic purpose of ECPD programs is to hire talented individuals who may not have the exact skills needed for a specific higher-level job and to train them over the course of several years so that they will develop the needed skills and expertise.

The merit-based federal hiring process is designed to ensure that the hiring process is unbiased and provides equal opportunity to all citizens. In particular, the system is designed to protect candidates against managerial exercise of arbitrary favoritism or discrimination. As such, the process emphasizes the evaluation of candidates based on their skills and their ability to *do* the job for which they are hired (see U.S. Merit Systems Protection Board, 1995). Under the traditional, competitive federal civil service hiring process, an entity with official hiring authority (such as OPM) or an agency with delegated examining authority (that is, a *delegated examining unit*, or *DEU*) rates and ranks applicants for the position according to job-related criteria,[8] This rating and ranking process also can assign additional "points" to applicants who are veterans. The competitive hiring process is designed to strike a balance between managerial discretion and objective notions of fairness in an environment where perfectly objective measures of candidate quality are difficult to come by. According to DoD managers with whom we spoke, this hiring avenue creates the biggest problems when there is a desire to consider candidates' potential for growth in addition to their ability to immediately perform the tasks

---

[8] See U.S. Merit Systems Protection Board, 1999, for a description of delegated examining authority.

required in entry-level jobs. The qualities that make a candidate more "desirable" to the hiring organization are often not the ones considered by the rating and ranking process for the specific job opening.

Three special authorities allow for noncompetitive appointments into civil service positions: the Outstanding Scholars Program, the Veteran's Recruitment Appointment Authority, and the Federal Career Intern Hiring Authority. However, each of these is limited in scope and does not apply to all positions and applicants.

Outstanding Scholars Program. This program allows federal agencies to directly appoint (a) qualified college graduates with a grade-point average of 3.5 or better or (b) graduates in the top 10 percent of their graduating class into certain positions at grade levels GS-5 or GS-7. Such outstanding scholars may be appointed without going through an examination process or the typical rating and ranking process. These positions are commonly described as "covered by the Luevano consent decree," in reference to the class action suit that led to the authority.[9] This hiring authority is intended for use as a supplement to, not as a replacement for, the standard, competitive examine methods of hiring.

The Outstanding Scholars Program may be used to hire individuals into positions at the GS-5 or GS-7 level that are classified at two-grade intervals and offer the potential of promotion to GS-9 or above. The range of job series covered by the consent decree is quite broad and includes many of the fields that would be considered in the general "business and management" area, including economics, personnel management, financial analyst, logistics management, and quality assurance specialist.

We found a great range in terms of the use of this authority by ECPD programs. At one extreme was a program that hires 90 percent

---

[9] The Outstanding Scholars Program was established in 1981 by a consent decree resolving a class action suit filed by Luevano et al. against OPM. The civil action claimed that a specific career exam required for entry into GS-5 and GS-7 positions in 120 occupations limited opportunities for Hispanic and African American applicants. The consent decree allows agencies to use the Outstanding Scholars Program to hire people into the positions that were covered by the lawsuit. It cannot be used to hire people into positions that were not covered (Office of Personnel Management, 2002).

of its ECPD participants through the Outstanding Scholars Program and believes that the quality of its program would be compromised if it had to rely solely on the traditional, OPM hiring process. At the other extreme were programs that have never used the Outstanding Scholars Program or were cutting back on their usage of it because of recent criticism that agencies are misusing it as a primary, rather than a supplemental, hiring authority (Saldarini, 2000; Office of Personnel Management, 2001).[10]

Veteran's Recruitment Appointment Authority. This option allows agencies to appoint individuals into positions at GS-11 or below without competition. It applies primarily to individuals who have served more than 180 days on active duty or were part of a reserve or guard unit serving in active duty during a period of war. Such veterans are eligible for VRA appointments within 10 years of leaving military service. Use of this hiring authority for ECPD programs is limited.

Federal Career Intern Hiring Authority. This authority, created by Executive Order 13162, July 10, 2000,[11] allows federal agencies to appoint individuals to two-year excepted service positions. It may be used only for positions that have a structured training component; upon successful completion of the traineeship, participants may be converted to competitive positions. This authority has provided a welcomed flexibility to some ECPD program managers but is less than perfect for positions covered by the Luevano consent decree. Candidates for those positions must still complete an assessment approved by Administrative Careers With America, and agencies must rank the candidates numerically. Several ECPD program managers reported that the Federal Career Intern Hiring Authority was particularly useful in hiring people for engineering and scientific positions, but that it is useless for positions covered by the Luevano consent decree. Indeed, many DoD agencies advise their staffing

---

[10] OPM has argued that federal agencies are overusing the program, which was originally intended to be a supplement to the regular competitive hiring process.

[11] See http://www.opm.gov/EO/13162.htm.

personnel not to use the hiring authority for positions covered by Luevano.

Another potential route for appointments into ECPD programs is through noncompetitive conversions from SCEP, which was discussed earlier in this chapter. ECPD program managers with whom we spoke were not making active use of this hiring avenue.

Presidential Management Intern Program. Established in 1977 by Executive Order 12008, and subsequently modified by Executive Orders 12364 and 12645, the Presidential Management Intern (PMI) program provides for the excepted service (Schedule A) appointment of up to 400 individuals per year into what are considered prestigious trainee positions in federal agencies. OPM administers the program, screening applicants and appointing them to positions in federal agencies, so this hiring authority is technically not directly available to DoD managers. Moreover, the program is very small (in 2003, DoD welcomed 17 PMI trainees). Candidates for the program are nominated by colleges and universities. Agencies such as DoD submit position announcements to OPM, participate in PMI job fairs, and interview PMI candidates. Agencies must reimburse OPM for the costs associated with recruitment, selection, screening, orientation, and graduation of PMI interns (approximately $5,000 per intern). Those who successfully complete their internship can be noncompetitively converted to competitive civil service positions.

Hiring for ECPD Positions Covered by Luevano

ECPD program managers expressed special concern about their ability to hire people into ECPD programs for positions covered by the Luevano consent decree. As discussed above, the Outstanding Scholars Program has recently been subjected to substantial scrutiny (Office of Personnel Management, 2001), and many managers we spoke with view the competitive process as the only viable hiring process available for positions covered by Luevano. Under the current competitive hiring process, OPM ranks candidates for an ECPD position according to specific job-related criteria and special preferences such as that for veterans. OPM then passes on to the program managers information on the top three candidates only. Managers must select one of the three if they wish to hire for that vacancy. This is referred to as the "rule of three" (U.S. Merit Systems Protection Board, 1995).

All managers noted that the process limits managerial discretion in hiring. In particular, it limits managers' ability to reject candidates based on any negative impressions they get during the interview process. An interview sometimes makes it clear that the candidate is not as strong as he or she looks on paper. More often, however, what is revealed is that the candidate is a bad match for the position. However, because managers are limited to three candidates per vacancy, they have very little opportunity to act on information from the interview process.[12]

Several ECPD program managers noted that the rating and ranking procedure is particularly problematic for ECPD programs. The purpose of ECPD programs is to bring people in at entry level and develop them into the workforce of the future. However, the rating and ranking process, which looks at job-related experience in its ranking, is not favorable toward young, smart people who are just graduating from college. As one manager noted, a veteran with a compensable service-connected disability who is on the verge of retirement and has many years of experience in an area only weakly related to the position will always be at the top of the list. Indeed, the average age of ECPD program participants is over 40 for several programs.

ECPD program managers expressed vastly different attitudes toward the competitive hiring process, reflecting the underlying tensions between the merit system principles and, on one hand, a federal commitment to provide preference in hiring to veterans, and, on the other hand, the desire for more managerial discretion. Some manag-

_____

[12] Such criticisms of the "rule of three" are not unique. Indeed, OPM itself has been advocating for changes to this approach, noting that it is a relic of the Grant administration and can arbitrarily limit managerial choices (U.S. Merit Systems Protection Board, 1995). The Homeland Security Act of 2002, responding to such criticism of the approach, allows agencies to substitute more-flexible categorical ranking procedures that have already been tested in selected agencies. OPM is developing guidance for the implementation of these flexibilities. (General Accounting Office, 2003; Friel, 2002.)

ers said the federal hiring process was an enormous barrier and that the ECPD program would fall apart if it were not for the Outstanding Scholars Program.[13] Other program managers viewed the hiring rules as essential for sustaining the larger federal goals of fairness and veterans' preference, but had developed strategies to make the process more flexible.

One such strategy is to centralize hiring at higher levels of the organization so that one "list" is being used to fill several vacancies. According to the "rule of three," if a selection entity is filling 10 positions, it can receive information on 30 candidates. It must then fill those positions from among the 30 candidates, but it is no longer limited to just the top three. In addition, for every offer made, the entity can call up an additional candidate on the list. Indeed, it need not make an offer to any of the top three candidates in this case. By grouping vacancies in this way, managers can dip deeper into the applicant pool in making their choices. This reduces the likelihood that a few unattractive candidates will block the applicant pipeline and prevent hiring.

Even when candidates are grouped, however, managers can be faced with having no option but to hire an individual whose interview suggested he or she might not be a good match. Some managers reported that, in such cases, they often take a risk on the candidate and then make use of the probationary period for competitive service employment, firing the individual if he or she does not perform well.

A final strategy that ECPD program managers use to focus attention on recent college graduates is to shorten the time window in which applications will be accepted and notify students who have been recruited through on-campus recruiting efforts about the job opening.

In sum, we find a complex hiring landscape for ECPD programs in DoD. The Federal Career Intern authority is an excellent tool for

---

[13] ECPD program managers are not alone in criticizing aspects of the federal hiring process. A recent GAO study (General Accounting Office, 2003) raised concerns about the rule of three as well as a key assessment tool used to evaluate candidates applying for positions covered by the Luevano consent decree.

ECPD program managers seeking to fill positions not covered by Luevano, since a structured ECPD program almost always meets the conditions for appointment via this authority. However, the options open to managers seeking to fill ECPD programs covered by the Luevano decree are more limited, particularly in view of attacks on the Outstanding Scholars hiring authority. Many managers continue to use the Outstanding Scholars authority in spite of the attacks, seeing it as essential to the success of the ECPD program, but some agencies are advising managers not to use it at all.

Mentoring Participants and Developing Programs
Mentoring is an explicit part of ECPD programs, although the responsibility for mentorship can vary. At Ford, the operating units are responsible for assigning mentors and developing the individual programs. Mentoring and evaluation of DoD ECPD participants are usually left to the local managers, although many DoD programs provide centralized guidance, training programs for supervisors, and even centrally developed evaluation tools.

Mentoring relationships can be formal or informal. The Army Career Intern Program delegates mentorship responsibilities down to the command level, and each trainee is assigned a local mentor. This program is well organized, despite the fact that intern managers receive no formal training. (One of the few things that interviewees mentioned they would like to do if given more resources was to have an orientation for managers/mentors.) Compared with pre-employment intern programs in DoD, DoD ECPD programs have more-formal mentoring arrangements. However, these arrangements still fall short of state-of-the-art in mentorship, as elaborated in the literature on best practices (see Chapter Three).

For ECPD programs, training program development is more or less centralized. In both DoD and the private sector, there is top-down pressure on traineeship content. The amount of training flexibility left to the discretion of the local manager and the trainees themselves will vary depending on the specific program. DoD ECPD programs often create a "template training program," which the career fields can adjust or expand upon as needed. For example, DFAS's

Entry Level Professional Accountant (ELPA) program has a detailed set of guidelines for training and professional development for program participants. Usually, the functional community provides input to the development of these templates. In addition, the templates include some courses or experiences that all interns should receive and thus that the career fields have little flexibility to adjust.

Evaluating Programs and Participants

The evaluation of ECPD programs can be centralized or decentralized. In DoD ECPD programs, evaluation tends to occur at the level responsible for funding the program. Ultimately, program evaluation is a tool for justifying the program's budget. Centralized programs have centralized, servicewide, or agencywide program evaluations. Depending on the size of the program, these evaluations can range from extremely data oriented and frequent to informal and infrequent.

Some evaluation efforts are highly complex. Perhaps the most sophisticated example we observed was the evaluation used for the Army Career Intern Program, a program closely tied in with Army civilian workforce planning efforts. Using an Army-wide personnel database that identifies whether an individual participates in the Army Career Intern Program or another locally or functionally funded intern program, analysts can compare the careers of those who participate in the Army program with the careers of those who do not. Analysts compared the career trajectories of two groups that had entered journeyman-level positions in 1974—one group that had been interns, and one that had been hired directly into the position. Among those who had been interns, 60 percent were still with the Army 25 years later; among the direct hires, only 35 percent were. The Army has also been looking at a similar "matrix" for later cohorts, allowing a comparison of first-year retention, second-year retention, third-year retention, etc., for later cohorts. To date, the finding is that the patterns have remained more or less the same over time. The Army also analyzed rates of promotion into management positions and found that interns are more likely to be promoted into such positions. For example, among those hired into journeyman-level positions between 1980 and 1990, the 10-year retention rates for Army Career Intern program graduates were 11 to 23 percent higher than those for other new hires, depending on the cohort examined.

About five years ago, the Air Force did a similar study on the retention of interns who went through centrally funded programs. It found that 58 percent of Palace Acquire interns and 62 percent of Copper Cap interns were still with the Air Force. This analysis was based on numbers over the programs' 18-year existence. The study also compared the careers of Palace Acquire and Copper Cap interns with those of interns who took part in locally funded programs. This analysis revealed no differences in retention or speed of promotion between the two groups during the internship. It did, however, find that, over the longer term, the Palace Acquire interns were more quickly promoted to GS-13 and received better performance ratings.

We found the evaluation of ECPD programs in DoD to be more advanced than the evaluations being done in the private sector, although private-sector managers did express interest in performing such analyses of their programs. However, as with the evaluation of pre-employment intern programs, the evaluation of ECPD programs suffers from inherent limitations. One such limitation is selection bias. Although it is instructive to compare the careers of those who participate in an ECPD program with similar cohorts of new hires who do not, it is difficult to attribute any differences to the ECPD program itself. Such claims can only be supported if those who do and do not participate in the program are the same in all respects except for participation in the program. In reality, hiring processes for ECPD programs differ from those for direct hires. As a result, those hired into ECPD programs may be different—in ways not observable in the data—from those hired into regular positions. For example, program participants may be more ambitious and career oriented than direct hires are, or more committed to having a career in the organization. It is possible that an organization might be using an ECPD program as both a recruiting and a training tool—that is, as a vehicle for both attracting better people and helping the organization retain them and make better use of their skills. In this case, disentangling the selection and the program effects may not be a major concern.

Another limitation of even sophisticated evaluations of ECPD programs is that the organization may treat direct hires and individuals who have "graduated" from ECPD programs differently. In other words, regardless of whether the program graduates are actually higher quality or have indeed acquired additional skills through the program, they may be perceived as such simply because they participated in a program the organization holds in high esteem. Indeed, the manager of one ECPD program reported that the organization at one time considered restricting promotions into certain types of positions to individuals who had gone through the ECPD program. This idea was ultimately rejected, but it nonetheless reflects the way in which organizations may become biased toward program participants. If this is the case, it is impossible to use comparisons such as those described above to evaluate the success of ECPD programs.

Facilitating Participant Migration to Full Performance

Decisions concerning whether to keep an ECPD participant on as a permanent employee are typically made with at least some input from the unit or functional area in which the employee will be working.

The process of transitioning DoD ECPD participants into permanent positions takes place at the organizational level that funded the program. In theory and if all goes well, ECPD participants are expected to continue working full-time at the location that sponsored them for the ECPD program. The centralized program asks local managers to commit to hiring the program graduates, in exchange for which they get the trainees for two to three years at no direct cost to their activity; the costs are covered centrally. However, there are various reasons why a local organization may not be willing or able to hire a trainee full-time, in which case, the central program office tries to place the person elsewhere.

At Ford, the ECPD program is decentralized to the level of the operation unit, and managers of these units take responsibility for structuring placement opportunities for individuals as they progress through the FCG program. Ford has no formal system for movement between operational units, however, so if an operational unit is reducing employment or the available positions are not in the participants' preferred locations, there is no automatic procedure for placing the FCG program participant or graduate in another operational unit. Also, although program participants do not sign formal mobility agreements, it is widely understood that continued employment is not guaranteed unless an individual is willing to move to where the jobs are.

Summary of Organizational Options for Intern Programs

ECPD Programs Are More Likely to Be Centralized and Formal

ECPD programs are more likely than pre-employment internships to be centralized and formal, in terms of both funding and program development. Because ECPD programs usually have broad firm- or agencywide goals, centralization is more likely and is appropriate to those goals. For pre-employment internships, training program content is often left to the discretion of operational managers, who may or may not receive significant centralized guidance. In contrast, program content in ECPD programs is almost always more regulated and formal.

In both DoD and the corporate world, part-time intern programs and co-op programs are decentralized and locally driven. Funding for these programs tends to come from local budgets and local personnel authorization. Participants are hired to perform local functions, and there is no central tracking or evaluation of program participants. Successful participants may be hired locally or, upon recommendation from the local contact, into an ECPD program.

Different Levels of Organizational Control Can Create a Structure of Conflicting Incentives

Different levels of organizational control or responsibility for pre-employment and ECPD programs create a structure of potentially different incentives for those involved with the management and administration of the program (though not for the interns themselves). For example, parties who get involved in intern program activities may have a variety of loyalties or affiliations within the organization. The first of these affiliational issues stems from the fact that individuals involved in a particular intern program may not all be associated with the same layers of the organizational hierarchy. Within DoD, this means some might work for an OSD-level office while others work in an office within Army headquarters, or in a service major command office, or for an individual installation. In the federal government, there is a hierarchical level that even goes beyond the DoD boundary in that OPM regulates the hiring process for all federal agencies. Similar hierarchical layers exist in private corporations, where an individual may perceive his or her primary affiliation to be with headquarters, a regional office, an operational unit, or a local plant.

In addition to a hierarchical affiliation, individuals involved in an intern program may be affiliated with a function or an occupation. An important distinction here seems to be whether the individual is part of the HR function or an operational function. There is also the issue of whether the individuals involved are specifically affiliated with and employed by the intern or ECPD program itself. Moreover, one individual may have multiple loyalties at any given time. For example, an individual may work in an HR capacity at the headquarters level or at the local installation level.

The degree of centralization of an intern program can also affect the breadth of goals. Centrally funded programs take a higher organizational view; corporate exposure is likely to be broader, and "success" is likely to be measured as the migration of an intern to *any* permanent position in the organization. Local or functionally funded internships, on the other hand, are more likely to correspond (though they need not do so) with parochial training and goals. The experience and training an intern receives are likely to be narrower and more locally specific, and a "success" for a location or function is seen as migration of an intern to a permanent position *in that location or function*.

The Locus of Funding for a Program Typically Drives Program Objectives

As we have seen, there are several models for funding pre-employment intern and ECPD programs. One clear conclusion from our research is that the locus of funding for the program drives or is reflective of program objectives. This is not surprising. An organizational entity that is supporting a program financially will see that its objectives are being achieved through the program. In addition, such an entity will bear some responsibility for ensuring that the program's graduates are being used in a manner that it deems effective.

Programs funded at a very high level, such as a military department or a corporate headquarters, tend to have the broadest aims, such as developing the future leaders of that service or company. Programs seek out individuals who are mobile and subject them to fairly broad training. The challenge such programs face is that local managers and even functional communities often do not feel any attachment to or responsibility for such program participants. In some cases, these managers and communities may not be willing to hire the program participants into specific positions upon program completion. In other words, these high-level programs can be detached from real operational hiring needs at the entry level.

Programs funded by a subunit of a larger service or agency tend to be more focused on that subunit's needs. Training and rotational assignments may espouse broader goals, such as the development of future leaders, but their focus is on a specific operational area or location. Another option is to leave professional development to local managers. In this case, the managers use their local budget to fund the training and recruiting programs needed to staff their activities.

The case studies and the literature on best practices suggest that some moderate level of centralization is a particularly effective option for funding pre-employment intern programs and ECPD programs that benefit a larger organizational subunit or the organization as a whole. If the program's benefits reach beyond a specific operating unit, a program structure that imposes most or all program costs on the local operating unit managers will likely lead to suboptimal use of the programs. Local managers already bear the cost of mentoring or working with program participants, so asking them to also pay for the direct cost of such programs is asking them to bear an additional burden. There is general recognition that a new entry-level hire will not immediately be a "jack-of-all-trades" who can quickly move into high-level management positions. Rather, new hires are seen as having to spend several years developing skills in a functional community or an organizational subunit. A functionally oriented and funded pre-employment intern or ECPD program, for example, provides the functional community some ownership over and responsibility for program participants. The functional community will more carefully consider its demand for these programs if it must pay the bill and place program participants. At the same time, a functional community may be better able than a local manager to deal with the risks and uncertainty involved in workforce planning, and to keep broader organizational goals in mind. Very discriminating central hiring might mitigate this tension, as would central hiring that allows input from the functional community.

Larger, More-Centralized Programs Tend to Have More-Comprehensive Program Evaluations

Our research suggests that the larger, more centralized programs tend to have more-comprehensive, or formal, program evaluations in place. This may reflect the fact that larger programs can take advantage of economies of scale when performing evaluations and that smaller programs, which cannot, find it difficult to justify the expense. However, this argument cannot be supported if several smaller organizational subunits with similar programs could use the same tools to evaluate their programs and jointly contribute to the development of those tools. Another reason that smaller programs might not have formal program evaluations is that informal evaluations may suffice for the smaller scale. The manager of a small program may not need to perform large-scale data analyses to track the careers of participants and compare them with nonparticipants if the organization is small enough that the manager knows what becomes of all participants.[14]

Be it formal or informal, program evaluation tends to focus on cost and some measure of whether the program is achieving its objectives. For pre-employment intern programs, the outcomes of interest are the percentage of interns who receive a permanent job offer, and the percentage of those receiving a permanent offer who accept that offer. ECPD programs tend to focus on the differences in retention and relative career success between program participants and similar employees who did not participate. Retention rates and time to promotion to certain high-level positions are common outcomes of interest.

Well-Regarded Intern Programs Are Part of an HR Structure Designed to Meet Organizational Goals

Although there is ample literature describing specific best practices used by successful intern programs, it appears that success may have more to do with the way programs are structured and with high-level support for such programs rather than with the use of specific practices. We found that the most important lessons for intern programs have to do not with the specific practices of programs, but with how programs are structured and located within the organizational structure. The intern programs that are well regarded by college counselors and by the business literature in general are part of an HR structure designed to serve functional aims. Successful programs are not owned and run by HR, but, instead, are supported by HR and receive significant input and funding from the functional communities and operational managers.

Centralization issues can be best resolved in a variety of ways, all of which involve centralization of some, but not all, activities. It appears that successful intern programs centralize activities that can

---

[14] Of course, there are many reasons why formal data analysis may be useful even in the case of small programs. First, informal observation may fail to recognize important trends or patterns. Second, informal observation will create evaluation challenges when the current manager leaves the organization.

benefit from economies of scale—for example, the design of evaluation standards and tools, training materials for mentors, and general guidelines for structuring the intern programs. In addition, it is common for organizations to centralize their contacts with colleges and universities to some degree.

However, functional communities typically play a key role first in identifying demand for interns (usually based on some medium-term forecasting of personnel needs in the functional area), selecting interns, designing the intern experience, and evaluating the intern performance. In other words, these activities tend to be less centralized in successful programs.

Lessons for DoD

Although DoD, like private-sector organizations, views pre-employment intern programs as a recruiting tool, DoD managers lack the degree of flexibility that allows the private sector to make offers of permanent employment to all categories of pre-employment intern program participants. Organizational structures that make migration to permanent positions appear easy and efficient to candidates also make recruiting from pre-employment internships easier. As we discussed earlier, corporations view pre-employment summer internships as a recruiting and pre-screening tool for permanent hires. A key aspect of their ability to benefit from intern programs stems from their efforts to evaluate program participants and make offers of employment to the most successful participants.

DoD does not currently have the ability to act on the information obtainable from a summer intern program. Specifically, there is no mechanism through which DoD can offer employment to interns who have completed only one summer program without requiring those interns to re-apply through the formal OPM competitive hiring process. To the extent that existing DoD hiring authorities and options limit or constrain migration, DoD is disadvantaged in the marketplace.

Organizational issues may also impede effective use of pre-employment intern programs as a recruiting tool. In DoD, pre-employment internships are local or sometimes functional in nature. Funding and all other key activities are controlled by local managers, sometimes with functional guidance. With the exception of the new Air Force effort to centrally fund 250 co-op students, we saw no examples of centralized funding for pre-employment internships or a link between pre-employment intern programs and ECPD programs. DFAS provides an example of business line, or functional, support for pre-employment intern and ECPD programs that may aid in recruiting at several different locations.

Within DoD, there is a strong local link between participation in a part-time intern program and hiring, since successful participants are eligible for direct conversion to a permanent position under SCEP hiring authorities. However, since the hiring is typically local, the ability to find employment for a participant if the local SCEP sponsor is unable to hire is limited.

In the next chapter, we consider DoD's options for its intern programs in our presentation of conclusions and recommendations.

CHAPTER FIVE

Conclusions and Recommendations

Conclusions

DoD has the full array of intern programs: summer intern programs, part-time intern programs, co-ops, and ECPD programs. However, DoD tends to use ECPD programs much more frequently than it uses the three pre-employment internship options. In addition, DoD agencies primarily use the term *intern program* to refer to ECPD programs. This terminology is potentially confusing to candidates, who typically view internships as a job preview opportunity for students rather than an actual permanent job.

Our review of the literature and of existing programs suggests that pre-employment intern and ECPD programs serve different purposes and that organizations often have both types of programs. Pre-employment intern programs focus on recruiting and screening potential employees, whereas ECPD programs provide training and professional development to employees once they are hired. Certainly, corporations that offer ECPD programs use them—and the implied opportunity for career advancement—as a selling point, but recruiting is not the primary aim of ECPD programs.

In private-sector organizations that offer both pre-employment internships and ECPD programs, the two are often closely linked and structured in similar ways. These organizations use their pre-employment intern programs to recruit for and staff ECPD programs. The reasoning is simple: If an organization is going to invest heavily in the training and development of a new employee through an ECPD program, then there is a potentially high payoff from carefully recruiting and screening those who will enter the program. Within DoD, we saw only one example, DFAS, in which ECPD and a pre-employment intern program were closely integrated. What is most common within DoD is for intern programs to be highly decentralized, ECPD to be more centralized, and the two types of programs to have little interaction. In other words, pre-employment intern programs are being used to help DoD recruit for and screen potential new hires, but only in a decentralized way and generally not in coordination with ECPD programs.

Whereas summer internships appear to be the most common form of pre-employment intern program in the private sector, DoD has relatively few summer intern programs and more part-time intern programs and co-op programs. We conclude that this is a rational response on the part of DoD managers given the hiring authorities available to them. Within the current array of hiring authorities, no option allows DoD managers to offer successful summer interns a permanent job after one summer. Such interns have no alternative but to apply through the regular, competitive hiring process open to all applicants. And then it is quite possible that they will not make the "rule of three" cut, which means the manager who sought to hire them will not be able to.

We were disappointed to learn that it is not possible to use the DoD civilian personnel master file to systematically track the careers of individuals who participate in DoD pre-employment intern or ECPD programs. However, because some individual DoD services and agencies do track such information, some findings were available to us. These suggest that ECPD program participants have higher retention rates and higher rates of promotion to senior management positions than do individuals who are hired into similar positions but do not participate in such programs, and that existing DoD pre-employment intern programs have conversion rates similar to those of private-sector organizations.

DoD would benefit from access to data that allow it to track the career paths of individuals who participate in pre-employment intern and ECPD programs in DoD. As we emphasized earlier, however, even with access to such data, the evaluation of intern programs faces serious challenges. Conversion rate is a useful piece of information for evaluating pre-employment intern programs, but it is not always an accurate or complete measure of program success. Moreover, internal organizational practices and selection bias can make it difficult to identify a "pure" effect of an intern program on career success.

We found the evaluation of ECPD programs to be more advanced in DoD than in the private sector. Specifically, the Army Career Intern Program has conducted extensive evaluations of the careers of program participants and has compared them with the careers of noninterns hired into similar positions. Using additional data available in the civilian personnel master file, similar analyses could be conducted for all DoD programs, allowing for comparisons across programs and consideration of mobility across organizational boundaries within DoD.

Our research suggests that program structure may be more important than specific practices. Successful pre-employment intern and ECPD programs are organized to meet company or agency goals. How the funding, recruiting, hiring, mentoring, program development, migration, and evaluation activities are organized is critical.

For each of those activities, there are certain advantages and disadvantages to centralization. Centralization works best when there are advantages to economies of scale or when the program's objectives are more congruent with the objectives of the organization as a whole rather than some part of the organization. The level of centralization of funding is particularly important, because goals and the perception of "success" often follow funding. Some of the difficulties associated with centralization can be avoided if operational managers and representatives from the functional community are involved in the centralized process (a hybrid approach). Ideally, pre-employment intern and ECPD programs will have commitment at all engaged levels.

We also found that well-regarded programs tend to be part of a larger HR strategy. Such programs are designed to meet a well-defined HR objective, such as enhancing recruiting or professional development.

Recommendations

Our analysis of internship programs within the private and public sectors led to several recommendations for DoD.

First, to more effectively recruit recent college graduates, DoD should develop and employ terminology for describing different programs that is free from DoD-specific jargon and consistent with terminology used in the private sector. Specifically, DoD should consider eliminating the use of the term *intern program* to describe bona fide, permanent jobs that involve a substantial amount of professional development. Students, particularly those not familiar with the federal government, will tend to assume that an internship is not a "real job." We have used the term *early career professional development* (ECPD) to describe these positions. DoD should consider adopting this or similar terminology. Several DoD agencies have developed program names specific to the agency or the career field (e.g., the Entry Level Professional Accountant program, the Navy's Financial Management Trainee program). Unfortunately, an important hiring authority available to managers of such programs, the Federal Career Intern Authority, uses the term *intern*. However, DoD should not let the name of a hiring authority used by managers interfere with the way in which it describes ECPD programs to those outside of DoD and the federal government.

Second, to the extent that DoD seeks to use pre-employment internships as a recruiting tool, it should create high-quality pre-employment intern programs that maximize the potential for hiring talented interns as permanent employees. The SCEP hiring authority gives managers the opportunity to use pre-employment intern programs in a way that is consistent with the way they are used in the private sector—that is, as a hiring and screening tool. In cases where managers believe it would be useful to use pre-employment intern programs for recruiting purposes, DoD should bear in mind the lessons from the private sector on successful pre-employment internships. In particular, DoD must be sure to design interesting work experiences with high-quality mentors so as to make a positive impression on program participants. A poorly run pre-employment intern program can be worse than no intern program at all.

Expanded use of pre-employment intern programs should acknowledge recruiting as a primary goal and be closely linked with overall HR objectives. In creating new programs or expanding existing ones, DoD must balance local and departmentwide needs and link decisions with larger workforce planning goals. As we witnessed in the case studies, local and organizationwide intern programs often address different objectives. Implementation of new or expanded pre-employment intern programs should reflect the best practices discussed in Chapter Three for such programs.

Third, if DoD intends to use summer internship as a recruiting tool, we recommend that it advocate changes to the SCEP rules. Current SEEP regulations provide DoD managers with the flexibility to use summer intern programs to achieve a variety of HR objectives. However, current SCEP requirements limit the extent to which DoD managers can effectively use these programs as a recruiting tool. There are many reasons for DoD to consider using summer internships as a recruiting tool—for example, their potential for attracting a much broader pool of candidates than part-time internships or co-op programs can.

If DoD decides to increase its use of summer internships as a recruiting tool, it should advocate policy changes that reduce the number of hours required for direct-conversion eligibility under SCEP. Current SCEP rules give managers at federal agencies, including DoD, the flexibility to directly convert to term or permanent employment only those individuals who successfully complete 640 hours of service as students. If this requirement were reduced to 400 hours of service, it could be met by a full-time summer intern in one summer. Managers would then have the opportunity to convert promising summer interns to term or permanent employment if they chose to do so, and the first step in expanding the effective use of pre-employment intern programs as a recruiting tool would have been taken.

Fourth, we recommend that DoD promote closer links between pre-employment intern programs and ECPD programs. Many of the private-sector companies examined in this study use pre-employment intern programs as a means of identifying employees for ECPD programs. To the extent that both types of programs share the objective of identifying employees the organization sees as desirable, it is useful to reinforce the connections between them.

DoD presently has an impressive collection of ECPD programs and a wide variety of pre-employment intern programs. We have identified several challenges that DoD faces in terms of realizing its goals for these programs, and have drawn lessons from these DoD programs and comparable programs in industry. It is our hope that our findings and recommendations will contribute to the understanding and future use of pre-employment intern and ECPD programs as tools to better achieve DoD HR goals.

Finally, we recommend that DoD gather information on participation in pre-employment intern and ECPD programs as part of the DoD-wide civilian personnel master file to facilitate the evaluation of such programs. Using the civilian personnel master file, DoD can track the careers of any civil service employee. If pre-employment intern and ECPD program participants could be identified in the data set, it would be possible to examine conversion rates and compare career progression, promotion rates, and retention rates for program participants relative to employees who are similar but do not participate in such programs. Such comparative analytic tools are already in use within some DoD services and agencies.

Description of Case Study Programs

This appendix briefly describes the intern programs used by each of the organizations interviewed for this research.

Ford Motor Company

Ford Motor Company hires people as co-op students, interns, and entry-level hires (Ford College Graduates [FCG] program), and at mid-career and senior levels ("experienced professionals"). All hiring activities, including pre-employment intern and ECPD programs, are organized around eight functionally based operational units. In 2002, Ford hired only 1,600 salaried people. In a typical year, Ford hires 5,800 to 8,000. About 30 percent of Ford hires are entry-level, recent college graduates. Nearly all such hires are brought into the FCG program.

The FCG program is described on the Ford recruiting Website (http://www.mycareer.ford.com/CareerPrograms.asp). It is a structured two- to three-year professional development program whose purpose is to develop company leaders. Each operating unit has devised a different program within fairly narrow corporate guidelines. Most of the operational units have a two-year professional development program, although there is some variation in program length (e.g., the career development program in manufacturing can last up to five years). These developmental programs include rotational assignments and skill development opportunities for new hires. Some (such as information technology, or IT) include cross-functional assignments in other operational units. There is a seven-week hands-on "New Hire Orientation" for IT people. All of the operational units assign mentors to the program participants to guide them in selecting professional development assignments.

Ford has a highly centralized summer intern program and a slightly less centralized co-op program. The summer intern program was scaled back in 2003 to 300 to 370 participants, down from 1,200 to 1,500 in previous years. Internships are organized around operational units; individuals apply to and are hired by specific operational units. Interns are funded from operations head count, and program administration by HR is billed back to operations. Nearly all interns come to work during the summer (May to August) and are located at Ford headquarters (HQ) in Dearborn, Michigan. The co-op program is small; it has about 100 to 200 participants. This program is driven by plant demand. A co-op participant is funded through the individual plant location, and participants are part of the plant's head count.

Hewlett-Packard

Hewlett-Packard (HP) has an extensive pre-employment intern program. The vast majority of the company's interns are summer interns, but HP refers to anyone who is a full-time student and works for the company as an intern, so under that rubric also fall what we call co-ops and part-time interns. The summer program runs from 10 to 12 weeks; in any given year, HP may have as many as 300 interns at the corporate headquarters, cohorts of 20 to 50 in the regional offices, and groups as small as a single intern in some of the smallest offices. HP maintains a close relationship with 47 universities and recruits heavily for its intern programs at these schools. The company's broad program focuses on recruiting and training future employees, as well as cultivating good relationships with its 47 schools. HP tries to bring top-quality (i.e., "desirable") students back summer after summer and then hire them when they graduate.

Northrop Grumman

At Northrop Grumman, summer internships are decentralized to the line of business level (each has an employment center). Summer interns work on ongoing projects, take classes, and get an overview of the company. The intern program is considered a recruiting tool, as well as a way to get work done inexpensively. It is considered a success if the manager is happy, and especially if he or she wants to keep the intern on part-time during the year. Keeping a summer intern on as a part-time intern is helpful in that the intern's security clearance will have been maintained if the intern is eventually hired full-time.

The program offers many benefits to participants, including group "fun" activities that are an important part of the experience. Interns are assigned a recent hire as a "buddy" to help them get settled as well. Summer interns take classes, get overviews of the company, and so on. Participants do not receive housing but do receive a relocation lump sum; the buddy can then help the participant find housing and get settled in other ways. The intern program money comes from direct (project) or indirect (overhead) charges to the budget.

Central Intelligence Agency

The CIA centralized its recruiting activities in 1998. Prior to that time, recruiting was highly decentralized, with over 60 different organizations doing their own recruiting—attending college fairs, screening applicants, etc. Recruiting in this decentralized environment was widely criticized, and Congress ultimately pressured the CIA to make its recruiting more efficient. Specifically, there was pressure to centralize activities that did not need to be replicated across the organization. The centralization and the transition were difficult, but today, managers are happy with the quality (i.e., "desirability") of recruits and are happy to be able to devote more of their attention to the activities of their operational units. The CIA now has a centralized recruiting center that handles recruiting for pre-employment interns, ECPD participants, and other permanent hires.

A preponderance of new hires (55 to 60 percent) are entry- or developmental-level hires. A small portion of these (approximately 10 percent) are brought in through the pre-employment intern programs.

The CIA offers several pre-employment intern programs. Unlike other organizations, it does not make a clear distinction between summer interns, part-time interns, and co-op participants. Interns of each type make the same level of commitment to the agency and go through a similar selection process.

The CIA takes the selection process very seriously. Student employees go through a screening process equally as rigorous as the one used for permanent employees. The reason for this is that anyone who works at the CIA has to go through the same health screening, background checks, polygraph checks, etc. This process is very time-consuming and costly to the organization, which is why the CIA makes the up-front investment in rigorous initial screening.

The CIA offers the following pre-employment intern and ECPD programs:

Undergraduate Scholar Program. The goal of this pre-employment intern program, which is currently going through some changes, is to attract minority and disabled students. The program originally targeted high school students who were planning to major in computer science or electrical engineering. Students would be offered a scholarship that could be used for tuition and school supplies. In addition, students would work at the CIA during the summer. It was possible to be part of the program without getting a scholarship (that is, it was possible to work only during the summers). Any scholarship student had to promise to work 1.5 years for each scholarship year. The conversion rate for this program was pretty low (by CIA standards)—49 percent. The program is now being modified in two respects. First, college sophomores who are entering their junior year in college have now become the target. The logic is that those individuals have selected a major and are in a better position to determine whether the CIA might be an attractive option for them. Second, the career areas covered by the scholarship program have now been expanded to include accounting and other fields that might be useful agencywide.

Student Trainee (Co-op). In this pre-employment intern program, students alternate school and work, and participants must be enrolled in schools that support co-op programs. Otherwise, it is the same as the internship program described next.

Internship Program. Under this program, students must commit up front to spend two tours with the CIA. One tour equals 90 days (three months), although the CIA has shown that it can be a bit flexible about the length of the tour. Both tours can be in the summer, or one can be in the summer and the other during the regular school year (perhaps delaying the intern's graduation). The CIA requires students to commit to two 90-day tours because of the up-front investment it makes in terms of pre-employment screening. Because this screening is so in-depth, the CIA wants to have interns on board for a longer time.

Additional, Directorate of Operations Programs. Two additional pre-employment intern programs, for the Directorate of Operations (DO), were started in the past few years: the DO Undergraduate Student Intern Program and the DO Graduate Student Intern Program. Both are six months long, either January to June or July to December. The DO formerly did not hire student interns due to the agencywide requirements for screening and for longer tours. Now, however, the DO has set up its own program with different requirements, which, like the other programs, is run through the recruiting center.

The Professional Training Program. This is a formal ECPD program for entry-level hires in clandestine services. Participants must be recent graduates with a bachelor's or master's degree. The program is 18 months in duration; at the end of it, participants are assessed for movement into the Clandestine Services Trainee Program. This is the general ECPD program for most positions in the DO.

Department of the Navy (DON) Human Resources and Financial Management

The Navy has two ECPD programs. The first of these, the HR Career Development Program, is a small program serving a functional area needed throughout the Navy. The program is brand-new, has a target size of 15, and is being piloted with nine trainees. It is "competency based" and uses an online assessment tool to evaluate the competencies. At each location/rotation at which trainees serve, they sit down with the supervisor at the beginning of the rotation and complete the assessment for the competencies they are supposed to work on during that rotation. The assessment provides a list of things trainees still need to work on while there. At the end of the rotation, trainees go through this process again. If their assessments are complete, trainees get a certification and can move on. Trainees who do not assess out at an adequate level of competency are flagged for additional or remedial instruction in that competency until they pass.

The second ECPD program is the DON Centralized Financial Management Trainee Program, started in 1970. It averages 4 to 45 trainees per year and is a two-year program with rotational assignments. According to SECNAVINSTR 12400.5C, "The goal of the Centralized Financial Management Trainee Program (CFMTP) is to ensure a continuous flow of highly qualified, college-caliber employees into the DON's civilian financial management work force to meet future succession planning requirements."

Defense Contract Audit Agency

DCAA runs pre-employment internships out of its five regional centers. The vast majority of its interns work part-time on a year-round basis. DCAA has two types of interns: office help and business/accounting students interested in auditing. The program focuses on recruiting the latter to permanent positions upon graduation. The program is small (it averages 20 interns per year per region) and is coordinated carefully but informally by the regional HR offices.

Defense Contract Management Agency

DCMA only has a three-year tenure as an independent agency (it was formerly part of the Defense Logistics Agency [DLA]). As such, it has a very young ECPD program, a program that was conceived before the DCMA was split off from DLA. This three-year "keystone program" was piloted in 1999 with 19 trainees. Its current program target size is 200, and growing. The program covers the core specialties of DCMA, including contracting, quality assurance, and several kinds of engineering. DCMA has developed an extensive development plan calling for formal training courses and rotational assignments with clients in years one and two of the program. By their third year in the program, trainees are expected to have a full journeyman specialist level of skill and to be migrating toward their full-performance position.

Defense Finance and Accounting Service

DFAS has recently been reorganized around six primary business lines:

- Accounting
- Commercial pay
- Military and civilian pay
- Corporate elements, which includes policy, finance, public affairs, etc.
- Corporate resources, which includes HR, acquisitions, RM, equal employment opportunity (EEO), and field operations (support not directly related to mission)
- Technical support operations.

Of these business units, accounting is the largest. Current recruiting and professional development efforts focus on professional accountants who perform the DFAS core mission. DFAS has a structured summer intern program that was developed by the accounting line of business. SCEP authority was used to hire students into a summer intern program last year; next year, STEP will be used for the summer interns. There were 32 participants in 2002, and 37+ were planned for 2003. In addition, DFAS has a handful of people participating in the SCEP program in a typical co-op manner.

In addition, the accounting business line has developed structured professional development programs for people hired into entry-level, professional accounting positions. There are two separate programs, distinguishing recent college graduates from those who are internally promoted. The Entry Level Professional Accountants (ELPA) program is for new external hires, primarily recent college graduates. There were 34 participants in 2001, 55 in 2002, and 68 projected for 2003. The Developmental Entry Level Professional Accountants (DELPA) program is for DFAS employees who have been converted from accounting tech positions into entry-level professional accounting positions. A prerequisite for the program is 24 hours of college-level accounting coursework.

U.S. Air Force Palace Acquire and Copper Cap

The Air Force sponsors two centralized, servicewide ECPD programs that have been in existence for 18 years. Palace Acquire is a general program; Copper Cap specifically targets contract specialist positions. Current program intake is 350 participants per year, with plans to increase that to 550 per year by FY 2007. The purpose of the programs is to attract the best and the brightest and to develop the future leaders of the Air Force. These servicewide programs co-exist with ECPD programs sponsored by major commands and local sites. Air Force Materiel Command (AFMC), which employs about half of all Air Force civilians, has been particularly active in developing its own ECPD programs and recruiting strategies.

U.S. Army Career Intern Program

The Army Career Intern program is a centralized, Army-wide ECPD program aimed at developing future leaders and managers for the Army. It is structured around the more general career field management process in the Army. There are 22 career fields, or programs, in the Army, which cover 86,000 out of 220,000 civilian employees. An individual whose job is part of a numbered series covered by a career program is automatically part of that career program. Examples of jobs not covered by career programs are legal and medical positions.

The centralized ECPD program dates back to the 1970s. Before that time, the functional communities ran their own programs. At some point, they decided to contribute resources to a central organization that would streamline the hiring and funding process. The program, which supports participants in a two-year program, has an end-strength of just under 1,000 work years for FY 2003. The program is scheduled to expand over the next seven years.

Army Materiel Command

AMC has an ECPD program that is part of the Army Civilian Training, Education and Development System (ACTEDS). AMC also has a small pre-employment intern program called CREST (Career Related Experience in Science and Technology), which takes advantage of the SCEP hiring authority. CREST averages about 90 interns and has a conversion rate of around 50 percent. AMC has also reinstituted an older, "apprentice" program at depots for blue-collar positions. This is a four-year program with a mixture of classroom and on-the-job training. The first year is 75 percent classroom work; the fourth is almost all factory floor work.

Information Assurance Scholarship Program

The Information Assurance Scholarship Program (IASP) is author-
ized by the Defense Authorization Act. Its goal is to "encourage the
recruitment and retention of Department of Defense personnel who
have the computer and network security skills necessary to meet
Department of Defense information assurance requirements" (U.S.
Code Title 10, Part III, Chapter 112, Sec. 2200).

The IASP supports a scholarship program and a pre-
employment intern program. The scholarship program pays for tuition, books, and a stipend for graduate and undergraduate degrees for
current employees of the U.S. government (both military and civilian) and for college students who are candidates to become employees
of the federal government. Scholarships are available only for study at
specific schools, which include DoD-run schools such as the Air
Force Institute of Technology (AFIT), as well as public and private
universities such as Carnegie Mellon. The scholarship program targets
students in their junior year, and some seniors are accepted as well.
The program also includes grants to participating universities to develop information assurance programs and to partner with defense
colleges and universities. Program participants are offered work experience in the field of information assurance in federal government organizations. Recruiting for the scholarship/intern program is managed by the colleges and universities that participate in the program.
Students apply through and must be recommended by their school.
Recommendations are sent to an HR office in DoD for rating and
ranking. Then, local organizations review applicants and make selections, interviewing candidates if they want. Interns are hired as student trainees through the SCEP and are on leave-without-pay status
while in school. It is possible to be selected for an internship without
receiving a scholarship.

Scholarship recipients are obliged to serve DoD as a civilian employee or in military service (the first-year cohort included only people obliged to civilian employment). The obligation is one full year

(not including the internship) for each academic year of scholarship support. Otherwise, the student must reimburse the government for the cost of the scholarship support.

Interview Protocol

Introduction

My name is XXX and this is my colleague YYY. We are researchers at RAND. RAND is a private, nonprofit, public policy research organization with a long-standing research relationship with the Department of Defense (DoD). We have been asked by the Office of the Secretary of Defense to study recruiting approaches used by private- and public-sector organizations, including DoD, to gather information about the different recruiting activities used by DoD components and agencies and to describe best practices found within DoD, in other branches of civil service, and in the private sector. In pursuit of such information, we are conducting interviews, site visits, and meetings with a wide range of human resources personnel in DoD and in other organizations. We want to learn more about the way in which recruiting activities are organized, how they are funded and administered, and what their strengths and areas for improvement are. The more we learn about existing recruiting activities through these visits, the better we will be able to advise DoD regarding the type of support that could further enhance the recruiting of civil service personnel.

Your participation in this interview is voluntary. Please feel free to tell us you don't know or don't wish to answer a question, or don't want to complete the interview.

Do you agree to participate in this interview?

Can we mention the name of your organization and things we learned about your organization in our report? If not, we will provide general information on the type of business, but not the name of the firm, in describing practices.

I. Overview of Recruiting Activities

Q. How does your organization break up or categorize different recruiting activities?
P. By field or area of expertise required?
P. By career experience, experience required?
P. By educational level?
P. By duration of employment term?

Q. Do you have specific programs or avenues through which hiring and recruiting occur?
P. Intern programs?
P. Co-op programs?

Q. How many people did your organization hire in the most recent year for which data are available?
P. What proportion of those new hires were entry level?
P. How many intern program participants did you have?
P. How many co-op participants?

Q. How do these numbers compare to those for previous years?

Q. To what extent do you make use of head-hunting firms or organizations that screen job candidates? For what types of positions?

Q. Describe where responsibility and authority for recruiting and hiring decisions rest within your organization. What is the role of the HQ office? regional managers? local managers?

Q. To what extent are the following processes centralized (in terms of funding, responsibility, authority)?
P. Identifying and funding personnel needs?
P. Developing job descriptions?
P. Recruiting for available jobs?
P. Screening applications?
P. Selecting applicants?
P. Training and development?
P. Mentoring?

II. Intern and Co-op Programs

Q. Can you describe typical internships and co-op programs in terms of duration, time of year, location?
P. How were these decided?

Q. Do your intern and co-op programs target particular types of participants?
P. By field of study?
P. By race or gender?
P. By educational level?
P. By institution (by institution quality)?

Q. What are the primary goals of your intern and co-op programs? (Answer for each program if there is more than one.)
P. Recruiting? (for your office? your company? your agency? DoD? the Federal Civil Service?)
P. Training?
P. Building community ties?
P. Getting work done cheaply by students?

Q. How do you evaluate the success of your intern and co-op programs?

Q. Do you monitor outcomes? If so, what outcomes do you track?
P. Satisfaction of students?
P. Satisfaction of managers?
P. Percentage of interns who are offered a job?
P. Percentage of interns who accept an offer?
P. Career path of former interns?

III. Resources

Q. Who (what organizational level) budgets for your internship and co-op programs?

Q. What is the overall budget?
P. Is it a fixed amount per year, or is it per student?

Q. How many interns and co-ops do you have at one time?
P. How is that number determined?

Q. What costs are reflected in the budget?
P. Intern wage?
P. Cost of mentorship?
P. Supplies?
P. Special programs or training for interns?
P. Cost of recruiting interns?

Q. What perqs do you offer interns and co-ops (housing, re-location, student loan credit, etc.)?

Q. What factors limit the size of your intern program?
P. Money (e.g., to pay interns)?
P. Availability of high-quality candidates?
P. Availability of good mentors?
P. Availability of good work assignments?

IV. Selecting Interns and Co-ops

Q. Is there a formal process for identifying, screening, and selecting interns and co-op participants?
P. Describe the process.
P. What organizational levels have input and responsibilities at different stages of the process?

Q. Who makes the hiring decisions?

Q. What do you do to recruit interns?
P. Is the recruiting targeted (school-specific, field-specific, functional areas, etc.)?

Q. Is the organization satisfied with the type and quality of candidates it gets?

V. Managing the Internship Process

Q. How is intern and co-op oversight organized?

Q. What training do you have for intern and co-op managers/mentors?

Q. What incentives exist for employees to serve as managers or mentors for interns?

Q. Who decides what interns and co-ops will do (job assignments)?

Q. Is there a formal evaluation process for interns and co-ops?

Q. What use is made of evaluations?
P. Are they directly involved in hiring decisions?
P. Are they available to other offices/components?

P. How long are these records kept?

P. Do they factor into changes in the intern recruiting process?

VI. Hiring Interns and Co-ops as Full-Time Employees

Q. What proportion of your interns and co-ops do you make offers of full-time employment to?

Q. What proportion of these accept?

Q. How long before (or after) the internship is completed do you make an offer?

Q. Once you decide you want to hire an intern permanently, how long is it before you can make an offer?

Bibliography

Askew, L. (n.d.). "Co-op Program Gives Technical School Students Opportunity to Learn," Warner Robins Air Logistics Center Public Affairs, http://www.afmc.wpafb.af.mil/HQ-AFMC/PA/news/archive/2001/aug/Robins_Coopprogram.htm (as of 4/15/03).

Brooks, Jennifer E., and Jacqui Cook Greene (1998). "Benchmarking Internship Practices: Employers Report on Objectives and Outcomes of Experiential Programs," http://www.naceweb.org/pubs/journal/fa98/brooks.htm (as of 11/14/02).

Crumbley, D. Larry, and Glenn E. Sumners (1998). "How Businesses Profit from Internships," *The Internal Auditor*, vol. 55, no. 5, October, pp. 54–58.

Cunningham, Julie (2002). *NACE's Building a Premier Internship Program: A Practical Guide for Employers*, National Association of Colleges and Employers.

Department of Defense (2001). *Civilian Human Resources Strategic Plan*, Office of the Under Secretary of Defense (Personnel and Readiness), Office of the Assistant Secretary of Defense (Force Management Policy), http://www.cpms.osd.mil.strategicplan/strategicplan.html (as of 1/8/04).

Department of Defense (2003). *DoD Civilian Human Resources Strategic Plan, Annex B: FY 2003 Year of Execution Plan*, Office of the Under Secretary of Defense (Personnel and Readiness), http://www.cpms.osd.mil.strategicplan/strategicplan.html (as of 1/8/04).

Emmerichs, Robert M., Cheryl Y. Marcum, and Albert A. Robbert (2003a). *An Executive Perspective on Workforce Planning*, MR-1684/2-OSD, Santa Monica, CA: The RAND Corporation.

Emmerichs, Robert M., Cheryl Y. Marcum, and Albert A. Robbert (2003b). *An Operational Process for Workforce Planning*, MR-1684/1-OSD, Santa Monica, CA: The RAND Corporation.

Friel, Brian (2002). "'Rule of Three' in Federal Hiring May Get Tossed," *Government Executive*, http://www.govexec.com/dailyfed/0302/031902 b1.htm (as of 10/13/03).

General Accounting Office (2002). *A Model of Strategic Human Capital Management*, GAO-02-373SP, Washington, D.C., March.

General Accounting Office (2003). *Human Capital: Opportunities to Improve Executive Agencies' Hiring Processes*, GAO-03-450, Washington D.C., May.

Gold, Melanie (2001). "Colleges, Employers Report on Experiential Education," http://www.naceweb.org/pubs/spotlight/020101fp.htm (as of 11/14/02).

Gold, Melanie. (2002). "The Elements of Effective Experiential Education Programs," http://www.naceweb.org/pubs/journal/wi02/gold.htm (as of 11/14/02).

Jobweb (2002). "Internships, Co-ops, Practicums, and Externships: What's the Difference?" http://www.jobweb.com/Resources/Library/Intern Coop_Programs/default.htm (as of 1/15/04).

Levy, Dina G., et al. (2001). *Strategic and Performance Planning for the Office of the Chancellor for Education and Professional Development in the Department of Defense*, MR-1234-OSD, Santa Monica, CA: The RAND Corporation.

Nagle, Rhea A., and Mimi Collins (1999). "Workplace Education: A Survey of Employers on Experiential Education Programs," http://www.naceweb.org/pubs/journal/fa99/nagle.htm (as of 11/14/02).

National Association of Colleges and Employers (n.d.). "For Employers: Making the Most of Recruiting Resources," Benchmark Briefs, http://www.naceweb.org/infocenter/colrel/jo_page 6 (as of 8/13/02).

Office of Personnel Management (2001). "Outstanding Scholar Hiring Inconsistent with OPM Guidance," *Issues of Merit*, November.

Office of Personnel Management (2002). "Outstanding Scholar and Bilingual/Bicultural Programs (Luevano Consent Decree)," http://www.opm.gov/employ/luevano.htm (as of 11/11/02).

Oldman, Mark, and Samer Hamadeh (2002). *The Internship Bible*, New York: Random House.

Patterson, Valerie (1997). "The Employers Guide: Successful Intern and Co-op Programs: How to Build a Successful Program," http://www. naceweb.org/pubs/journal/wi97/patterson.htm (as of 11/14/02).

Saldarini, K. (2000). "Data Shows Decline in Outstanding Scholars Hires," *Government Executive*, February 14, http://www.govexec.com/dailyfed/ 0200/021400k1.htm (as of 1/15/04).

Scott Resource Group (1999). "Internship Program: Best Practices Revisited," January, http://www.scottresourcegroup.com.

U.S. Air Force (2003). "AFMC Work Force Shaping," Fact Sheet, http: //www.afmc.wpafb.af.mil/HQ-AFMC/PA/library/WFS_Fact_Sheet.htm (as of 4/15/03).

U.S. Merit Systems Protection Board (1995). *The Rule of Three in Federal Hiring: Boon or Bane?* A Report to the President and the Congress of the United States, Washington, D.C.: U.S. Merit Systems Protection Board, Office of Policy and Evaluation.

U.S. Merit Systems Protection Board (1999). *The Role of Delegated Examining Units: Hiring New Employees in a Decentralized Civil Service*, A Report to the President and the Congress of the United States, Washington, D.C.: U.S. Merit Systems Protection Board.

Watson, Bibi S. (1995). "The Intern Turnaround," *Management Review*, vol. 84, June, pp. 9–12.

Whitman, G. (n.d.). "Co-op Students Breathe Relief into Civilian Personnel Shortage," http://www.afmc.wpafb.af.mil/HQ-AFMC/PA/ news/archive/2002/mar/HQ_Coopstudents.htm (as of 4/15/03).